Cambridge E

Elements in Religion and Monotheism
edited by
Paul K. Moser
Loyola University Chicago
Chad Meister
Bethel University

MONOTHEISM AND RELIGIOUS DIVERSITY

Roger Trigg
University of Oxford

CAMBRIDGE
UNIVERSITY PRESS

CAMBRIDGE
UNIVERSITY PRESS

University Printing House, Cambridge CB2 8BS, United Kingdom

One Liberty Plaza, 20th Floor, New York, NY 10006, USA

477 Williamstown Road, Port Melbourne, VIC 3207, Australia

314–321, 3rd Floor, Plot 3, Splendor Forum, Jasola District Centre, New Delhi – 110025, India

79 Anson Road, #06–04/06, Singapore 079906

Cambridge University Press is part of the University of Cambridge.

It furthers the University's mission by disseminating knowledge in the pursuit of education, learning, and research at the highest international levels of excellence.

www.cambridge.org
Information on this title: www.cambridge.org/9781108714457
DOI: 10.1017/9781108637503

© Roger Trigg 2020

First published 2020

A catalogue record for this publication is available from the British Library.

ISBN 978-1-108-71445-7 Paperback
ISSN 2631-3014 (online)
ISSN 2631-3006 (print)

Monotheism and Religious Diversity

Elements in Religion and Monotheism

DOI: 10.1017/9781108637503
First published online: August 2020

Roger Trigg
University of Oxford

Author for correspondence: Roger Trigg, roger.trigg@theology.ox.ac.uk

Abstract: If there is one God, why are there so many religions? Might all be false? Some revert to a relativism that allows different 'truths' for different people, but this is incoherent. This Element argues that monotheism has provided the basis for a belief in objective truth. Human understanding is fallible and partial, but without the idea of one God, there is no foundation for a belief in one reality or a common human nature. The shadow of monotheism lies over our understanding of science, and of morality.

Keywords: diversity, relativism, transcendence, polytheism, toleration

ISBNs: 9781108714457 (PB), 9781108637503 (OC)
ISSNs: 2631-3014 (online), 2631-3006 (print)

Contents

1 One World

1.1 The Problem of Religious Diversity

Religious diversity brings with it a whole set of religious and philosophical problems. It must, however, be seen in the context of wider views of human diversity, and, indeed, of whether the adjective 'human' carries much weight. Is there is such a thing as 'being human' outside particular social contexts? For some, the very words 'difference', 'diversity', 'multiculturalism', 'tolerance', are clarion calls to accept the multifarious nature of human societies. Social variation seems far more salient than the fact that they have anything in common.

In the field of religion, in particular, this acceptance of difference can be made to seem naive and simplistic. To put it bluntly, when there are so many religions, why should any of them be believed as true? The invocation of the idea of truth jars against the happy acceptance of difference. Perhaps some, and maybe all, religious believers are deluded into accepting obviously false beliefs. Richard Dawkins, in one of his diatribes against religion, starts his argument with the fact of religious diversity. He says, in a chapter ironically entitled *So Many Gods!*, 'I don't believe in any of the hundreds and hundreds of sky gods, river gods, sea gods, sun gods ... so many gods to not believe in'.[1] He concludes, 'People growing up in different countries copy their parents and believe in the god or gods of their own country. Those beliefs contradict each other, so they can't all be right'.[2]

Dawkins, however, assumes that there is such a thing as being 'right'. Truth matters to him, and he holds that it is true that there is no God, or gods. There is, however, a temptation of long-standing not to make judgements about other people's beliefs, and even to assume that there can be different 'truths'. Yet that itself brings up the question of what reasons each person can have for particular beliefs. If truth is not of universal significance, perhaps we ourselves have little reason to maintain our existing beliefs. Why should we even imagine that there is an objective truth that all should aspire to? Yet, as we shall see, that idea is at the root of monotheistic religion, and it is transferred to modern science. It is an idea stemming from monotheism, but, paradoxically, used against it by atheists such as Dawkins.

How should we confront the fact of diversity? This is of particular importance in religion where, for many, diversity of religious belief presents as much an obstacle against faith, as, say, the venerable problem of suffering. Religious diversity is, however, part of a wider problem. It raises deep questions about the

---

[1] R. Dawkins, *Outgrowing God*, p. 6   [2] Dawkins, p. 10

possibility of human rationality, the role of human freedom and the accessibility of truth. No consideration of diversity should avoid these larger issues.

1.2 Diversity and Power

In the present age, diversity is celebrated more often than it is defined. At root is a horror, perhaps in the Western world stemming from post-imperialist guilt, of the imposition through power of one set of beliefs or practices over apparently alien ones. Difference, it seems, should be respected. A desire that everyone be like 'us' in our beliefs and practices appears intolerant, and probably racist. It seems to assume, illegitimately, our superiority over others. There is a conflation, often deliberate, between the views a person holds and the nature of that person. What is taken for knowledge or fact is allegedly the outworking of power structures. Appeals to truth become the mere imposition of power by one group over a weaker one.

An important step to this kind of analysis is the idea that there is no such thing as human reason, any more than the there is such a grouping as 'humanity'. There are instead multiple forms of rationality, different ways of reasoning. This may be unexceptionable. The methods of science, for example, may not be simply transferable to religion. Yet to suggest that there are different rationalities is another position entirely. If there is not a more basic set of rational capabilities, common to all human beings, different humans are cut off from each other. This results in a rigid distinction between different intellectual disciplines, different epochs, different races and so on. Alister McGrath, who himself still wants an ontological unity, has described the situation well when he refers to 'a growing realisation that both the beliefs we hold and the rationality through which we develop and assess those beliefs, are embedded in cultural contexts'.[3] One may wonder who 'we' are in this context. The use of the collective pronoun itself suggests a continuing commonality that the picture implicitly denies. The stress is on what he terms the 'historicity of rationality', and is distinguished from ahistorical thinking that assumes we can abstract people from their social context, and interrogate them as equals.

It is a basic assumption of much of the history of philosophy that there are sufficient points of contact between, say, Plato and Aristotle and ourselves to make the study of their work still relevant. The same reasoning applies to theology. If, for example, the New Testament operates with forms of rationality alien to ourselves, why study it? If the manner in which we sense and interpret the world is determined by influences which, by definition, may be beyond our knowledge and control, as some cultural influences could be, we are locked into

---

[3] A. McGrath, *The Territories of Human Reason*, p. 22

systems of thought which can have little overlap with each other. We see the world our way and others see it theirs, and it is easy to say how any idea of the unity of that world can be lost. We cannot think that we live in the same world our forbears did, so their views will not only be opaque to us, they are actually irrelevant to our needs and interests.

Much has been made in recent decades of the postmodernist reaction against modernist views of rationality, seen as the product of the Enlightenment. Beliefs vary across cultures, not least because available evidence about the world has varied. The invention of telescopes and microscopes provided an example of how available technology can be a crucial factor in the development of knowledge. Saying that the criteria of what is reasonable is culturally situated, however, means more. It suggests that human rationality is itself the product of time and place. The result will be a never-ending splintering of ways of understanding. Even an idea of modernity, with its universalist pretensions and challenged by postmodernism, can itself splinter. Many wish to turn from the idea of reason as an innate mental faculty, common to all humans, to a study of differing social practices. A common human hunger for the divine and the search for it, can be reduced to analysis of different forms of religious practice. The embedding of language in practices, and a recognition of different forms of life has been characteristic of the work of the later Wittgenstein. He has exercised a vast influence not just in twentieth century philosophy but also in such fields as social anthropology.

It is tempting to generalise one's own views and hold that they should be accepted by everyone everywhere. This is particularly true in religion where a universalising influence can lead, as we shall see, to intolerance and lack of respect for, or sympathy for, other religions and forms of religious practice. When we move our attention from what is real and true, to what is believed in all its multifarious forms, whether in religion or elsewhere, diversity can itself seem to be the ultimate fact. The focus moves from what beliefs purport to be about to the fact of the beliefs themselves. Once we convince ourselves that rationality cannot transcend difference but is itself constituted by diversity, everything becomes relative to culture. We are then culturally embedded and cannot aspire to a 'God's eye view', seeing things as they really are. We must recognise that our view is always from somewhere. Our interest has to be on the fact and location of belief rather than its target. The inescapable conclusion will be that, just as we cannot attain God's view, we can know nothing about God or the gods as they are in themselves. We are the creation of our cultures and everything will reflect that, including our theology or any understanding of what lies beyond our beliefs or is transcendent.

An illustration of this is the undoubted loss of confidence in the traditional foundations of Western culture. At times, the imposition of Western ways of doing things were at best silly, and at worst harmful, to those with their own traditions and customs. Does that, though, mean that Western standards of knowledge, however imperfect, were themselves never any better than those of colonial subjects? Were those who took Western medicine, and Western standards of schooling, to those who knew neither, merely guilty of imposing their standards on others? Should Western science and medicine have claimed no more for themselves than could the incantations of witch doctors? Were missionaries merely guilty of using imperial power to enforce their view of the world on others? If so, any claim to truth, in science, religion or elsewhere, becomes simply an exercise of power.

In any consideration of religion and diversity, we must ask whether even an assertion of monotheism is itself an exercise of power by some people. If carried to extremes, this attitude undermines all rationality, all understanding of any truth to be discovered, and all appreciation of a reality beyond us that can constrain our beliefs. All, as Nietzsche said, is interpretation. Who is right? The idea of being right has to disappear, along with all possibility of truth. All we are left with is the mere fact of diversity. That itself, however can no longer be seen as objective fact but is itself only constituted by our present social beliefs.

When the content of what is said is subordinated to the issue of who is saying it and their particular situation, it is not surprising that identity politics comes to the fore. Who I am becomes more important than what I might be claiming. The interests at work, it will be claimed, invalidate any idea that I could be engaged in the dispassionate search for what everyone should recognise is true. So-called intersectionality has spread its influence from sociology across the humanities. The idea has been that social inequality, for example, should not be explained merely by class, gender, or race alone. Yet as one writer on intersectionality has put it, such categories cannot themselves be fixed concepts. She insists that 'each of these social categories is fluid, contextual, and open to debate'.[4] Such social categories can themselves be seen as the operation of power structures. Hierarchies of power can be as potent in academic disciplines as anywhere else. Social identities are thus themselves seen as constructed. At each level of understanding – from ordinary interactions in society to the most abstruse level of sociological explanation – everything is reduced to the operation of power structures. They are at their most potent when unacknowledged, so denial of their existence can itself seem to give evidence of their potency. Once everything is explained in terms of 'systems of power, manifested in social

---

[4] M. Romero, *Introducing Intersectionality*, p. 6

relationships of dominance and subordination', we have totally undermined any possibility of explanation.[5] All is lost in an infinite regress of suspicion. We ourselves have nowhere to stand.

When all claims to truth and to understanding the world are controlled by ideas current in societies that are themselves merely controlled by the pursuit of power by a hegemonic group, the idea of truth must collapse. We are told that intersectionality is a tool for 'creating new systems of knowledge for greater understanding of domination and resistance'.[6] It attempts to unmask privileges obtained as a result of identities linked to existing systems of power. Yet at each stage, any assertion about alleged facts can be challenged as the mere expression of a system of power. Whenever humans can interact, as they do when they use language, they can be accused of using whatever position they hold as a subtle form of domination. The same approach can be levelled against the accuser, and then one is involved in a spiral of recrimination and claims of bad faith. Truth becomes inaccessible, as does any notion of the world 'as it is in itself'. All that matters is the identity of the person making the claims, and that itself will be contestable. Language becomes detached from the world and then can no longer be understood as referring to anything beyond itself. Its function as a means of communication is put in doubt. It even becomes unclear how a language can ever be learnt. We have to recognise and reidentify objects in the world around us and assume they are the same for everyone. We all live in one world, whatever its nature and extent, and, as humans, all normally have similar access to it. There is, it can be said, one human nature. That is why we can hope to understand people who may at first seem very alien.[7] We would not be able to make such an assumption about real aliens, such as the archetypal Martians. Even then we might be able to assume that since they were living in the same universe they were constrained by, and reacting to, the same physical world that confronts all human beings. Their 'nature' and sensory equipment could, however, be very different.

Such assumptions are put into question by forms of relativism that relate the idea of truth, and of reality, to the beliefs that may be held. Relativism, by its nature, cannot talk of what is the case without reference to who holds beliefs about it. The fact of belief becomes more significant than what the belief is about, or its content. Such relativism has a long pedigree, and Plato argued in his dialogue, *Theaetetus*, that it has to be self-contradictory. In the dialogue, Socrates portrays the sophist, Protagoras, as saying that each of us 'is a measure of what is and is not'.[8] 'Man is the measure of all things' in

---

[5] Romero, p. 114   [6] Romero, p. 58

[7] For more on understanding other cultures, see R. Trigg, *Understanding Social Science.*

[8] *Theaetetus*, 166d

Protagoras's famous dictum, and the doctrine was extended to whole societies. He said that 'whatever practices seem right and laudable to any particular state are so, for that state, as long as it holds them'.[9] Socrates then goes on to point out the Protagoras must admit that everyone's opinion is true (at least for the holders, we may add). Protagoras has to accept that if others reject his doctrine, his doctrine is false for them. Underlying this is the realisation that assertion in language involves claims to truth. If all claims to truth have to be relative, even relativism cannot coherently be stated, let alone claimed to be true. The relativists will in the end have to be convicted of saying something like, 'It is true there is no such thing as truth', or 'it is an objective fact about the world that there are no objective facts'.

Such relativism has sometimes been applied to science in what has been termed the sociology of knowledge. The result can be devastating. Science itself can be cut adrift from any claim about physical reality, because it is seen merely as the product of a particular culture. It can be dismissed as 'Western' science. Even more insidiously, it can be seen as part of some power structure conferring privilege on some and subordination on others. Post-modernism has been very adept at challenging the pretensions of science, and its claim to be operating a rationality that holds universally.

1.3 Different Religions

One reason that relativism is so easily accepted is our confrontation, given modern forms of communication, with the diversity of belief and practice that exists across the world. Nowhere is this more apparent than in the area of religion. It seems tempting for many to dismiss different religions as merely true for the particular believers but having no relevance to the rest of us. Yet this was a problem recognised by the ancient Greeks. Their polytheistic religion did not stand up to the rational scrutiny of thinkers from the very beginnings of philosophy. One of the so-called pre-Socratic philosophers, Xenophanes of Ionia, is known to us only in fragments of his thought. Writing around the beginning of the fifth century BC, he exposed the anthropomorphic character of any human understanding of gods, saying, for instance, that 'Ethiopians say their gods are snub nosed and black, Thracians that theirs are blue eyed and red haired'.[10] Xenophanes was not impressed by humans' ability to see gods in their own image. This stems from a general inability to think in terms other than those with which we are familiar. The result can be to relativise judgement and beliefs to the people holding them. Xenophanes claimed if horses had the ability to draw, they would picture gods as horses.

---

[9] *Theaetetus* 167c   [10] Xenophanes, fr 16 (in Kirk, Raven and Schofield)

Theological notions, even of a primitive kind, can then be judged as a projection of human characteristics. Xenophanes was certainly suspicious of anthropocentric reasoning, and was critical of traditional Greek polytheism as portrayed in Homer and Hesiod.[11] He saw the Greek gods as merely reflecting bad human characteristics, such as theft and adultery. Such portrayals come from a desire to understand the gods as possessing human traits, but to a greater degree than ordinary mortals.

Yet Xenophanes seemed to be pointing to a reality that should not be seen merely in human terms, nor as the reflection of the peculiarities of one society. One fragment has fascinated scholars, since he claimed that 'one god is greatest among gods and men, not at all like mortals in body or thought'.[12] That tears theology away from folk religion, and abstracts the nature of the divine from particular beliefs in particular places. Some have seen in the fragment the glimmerings of a monotheism that did become explicit in later Greek philosophy.

From the very beginnings of Western philosophy, a century before Plato or Aristotle, diversity of belief in general, and religious diversity in particular, caused problems. The more one concentrated on the fact of belief, the more the anthropocentric character of many religious beliefs was obvious. There was a greater knowledge of different customs and practices in different places. Philosophy, like all intellectual disciplines, tends to operate within a presupposition that there is a universal truth to be sought after. Yet the accusation that one is simply proselytising, so as to spread one's own belief system in religion or elsewhere, can be effective. How can anyone assume a position of omniscience so they can dismiss other people's beliefs? We have to face the philosophical question of what entitles us to believe that anything lies beyond the cacophony of conflicting beliefs, particularly in the field of religion. The challenge of which, if any, of all the diverse religions confronting us should be accepted still confronts us. Yet a genuine relativist cannot even acknowledge the objective fact of difference and diversity. What is different for us may be different from what is different for other people. We get caught in a never-ending cycle of incomprehension. It is been recognised in the philosophy of science and elsewhere that positing different worlds in whatever context must lead to an incommensurability between them. They cannot be compared. What counts as data in one world will not in another. Cogent evidence in one world will be ignored in another.

In what is now regarded as a classic in the philosophy of science, though still controversial, Thomas Kuhn in the 1960s introduced the word 'paradigm'. This

---

[11] Xenophanes, fr 11   [12] Xenophanes, fr 23

referred to the different conceptual schemes with which scientists operate to interpret the physical world after a so-called scientific revolution. An example would be the transition from classical to quantum mechanics. The result is that, as Kuhn claimed, 'after a revolution, scientists work in a different world'.[13] Certainly they see the world differently, but do they work in a different world? That makes reality depend on whatever beliefs happen to be held by scientists, and would undermine the possibility of genuine physical science. Common sense suggests that we live in a real world which is often resistant to our own efforts and intentions. We bump into things. Yet for Kuhn, and subsequent social constructivists even in the field of science, reality becomes a reflection of human belief rather than its target.[14]

If we believe in many gods, it can be said we live in a different world from those who believe in the one God. If we are atheists, we appear to live in a different world from either. Who is right? Yet no one can be. Everyone is justified within their own world by the terms of their own beliefs. There is nowhere external, no one real world, where anyone can even in principle stand. The post-modernist rejection of Enlightenment rationality ensures that, in some quarters, reason is seen as the product of the presuppositions of the particular world we inhabit. In science, there can be no neutral data or neutral evidence. Everything is already the product of a particular theory. An added ingredient for some is that all is governed by the cynical exercise of power. Nietzsche's influence lives on particularly in the work of the twentieth-century French post-modernist philosopher and social theorist, Foucault, who stressed the role of power. The inevitable result is the splintering of human understanding. There can be no common ground, and no way of translating one conceptual scheme, tradition or religion into another.

There is a truth in this. It is easy to interpret an alien religion in terms, say, that are familiar to Christianity but which fundamentally misrepresents it. It is wrong to assume that other religions are somehow inferior forms of Christianity, when they can be totally different. In similar fashion, it can be a mistake to assume, without qualification, that the motivations of characters in a novel of another epoch must be the same as ours. Twenty-first century fashions and conventions cannot be imposed on other eras without distortion. Historical sensitivity is required.

Does this surrender to the relativist? Maybe we are so imprisoned by the thought processes of our own religion or era that we can never shake them off. That would have to be so, if there was no common ground underpinning all

---

[13] T. S. Kuhn, *The Structure of Scientific Revolutions*, p. 134

[14] See R. Trigg, *Reason and Commitment*, ch. 5

human eras and traditions. We would then always merely see our own reflection, once we study other cultures or historical periods. The question remains how we can understand other religious beliefs when they are seemingly very different from our own. One answer must be that 'we' cannot be defined so narrowly as to be confined to place and time. We are human. Our sharing of a common nature, itself a basic anti-relativist assumption, gives a platform on which to stand. Otherwise, history would be impossible, as would attempts, such as social anthropology, to compare human beings in different settings.

We think we can still understand the words of the empiricist philosopher, David Hume, written in the eighteenth century. He championed the idea that human nature remains the same across nations and ages. He said: 'Would you know the sentiments, inclinations and course of life of the Greeks and Romans? Study well the temper and actions of the French and the English'.[15] We cannot be locked into the presuppositions of a particular age with its own conceptual scheme. The simple claim of the relativist is always that times change and that we must keep up with the times. To say that something is old-fashioned is to condemn it. Yet what marks one age or conceptual scheme from another? What defines them? How long do they last? Are the views of Foucault, published in the 1970s, now becoming incomprehensible to us, or can Nietzsche's strictures on power be ignored because they were written in the century before last? The nineteenth-century Nietzsche must then surely now be beyond our understanding. With rapid technological change creating new forms of communication and of society, does that mean that old people could not remember how they used to think? We cannot shut off one age from another. If we do, we limit our understanding, together with our ability to stand back from ourselves and assess our present situation.

A secular society may, through ignorance or indifference, find it difficult to empathise with religious people, but that does not make it logically impossible. There are myriad matters of disagreement and possible misunderstanding even between individuals. If we wish to be in a society with absolutely settled, shared assumptions, in which there is no disagreement, we are liable to find ourselves very lonely. We all, as individuals, differ from each other in some way.

1.4 The One and the Many

Despite our differences, we share a common human nature, which provides an important basis for mutual understanding. There is much in modern evolutionary biology that supports this assumption. Human beings use inter-translatable languages to communicate the same basic needs and interests. We share the

---

[15] *Enquiry*, ed. Selby-Bigge, p. 83

same biology, including common ways of perceiving the world. The mapping of the human genome in recent years has underlined the commonality that exists between all humans. Evolution may adapt humans to different ecological niches, but our common characteristics are rooted in our biological nature. The interaction of genes and environment can be subtle, but, as has often been said, the genes hold culture on a leash. They set limits that human cultures cross at their peril. As an extreme example, a culture (or religion), preaching youthful suicide or total celibacy, will not long survive.

Even so, the concept of human nature is questioned, and denied, in some quarters.[16] That, though, makes the idea of human genome having any influence on human behaviour very questionable and challenges much of the basis of biology. Indeed any reference to humanity, as such, has to be proscribed. Even the idea of human rights, however much they are invoked, is exposed as at best an arbitrary social construction, and, at worst, an illusion. There cannot be any human rights in virtue of our common humanity, if there is no common humanity. This denial of human nature is part of the wider denial of any independent reality existing apart from our conceptions of it. Yet the success of human thought does not just presuppose a commonality between thinkers and their access to the world. It assumes that we will confront the same world. The question still remains how we can understand it, and to what extent our limitations as human beings limit our understanding.

A necessary presupposition of science, let alone all human thought and language, is that it investigates an independent reality. The world of science is not constructed but discovered. It is an indispensable presupposition of science that there is one physical world that exists in the same way in different places. There is not an American world, a British world or a Chinese world. The world is one. By that, modern science does not just mean our everyday world. Its reach stretches to the whole universe, or even, as some physicists would have it, to a multiplicity, even an infinity, of universes. Some scientists even envisage our universe as one of many different universes which operate according to different physical laws. The unity of science, and of its capabilities must then be in jeopardy, since human science could never access, let alone understand, such absolute physical diversity. This illustrates how what used to be called the uniformity of nature is a presupposition underlying our ability to do science and enable it to progress. We must assume that what is valid here is valid there, that which is demonstrated now will obtain then. We can extrapolate because of a confidence that physical reality, wherever it is found, will possess the same enduring characteristics.[17]

---

[16] See R. Trigg, *Ideas of Human Nature*
[17] For more on this see R. Trigg, *Beyond Matter: Why Science Needs Metaphysics?*

This one world exists in its own right. Science is not a projection of human wishes or constructed out of whatever conceptual system we happen to have. It is a painstaking method of building up, by trial and error, and through theory and falsification, provisional understandings of the nature of the universe. Scientists, however, investigate *one* reality. Whatever the race, class, gender, religion or lack of it, of the investigator, that is all irrelevant. The content of a scientific belief, or the nature of a theory, may be influenced by its background for good or ill; It can never be validated by that. We all confront the same physical reality that exists independently of us. Our scientific theories are vindicated, or not, by the way in which they can attempt to unlock the secrets of the universe. They are tested by what actually happens and not by what we want to happen, or even assume must. Our search for knowledge is constrained by that reality. There are not different worlds for different scientists, even if they come from different cultures. The purpose of science is to tell us about what actually is the case. This is the reason why there is always a possibility for a clash with some religious claims, which may also be trying to tell us about the nature of an objective reality.

What there is and how we obtain knowledge of it must always be distinct questions. Epistemology cannot dictate ontology. There is an issue as to why human minds are attuned to the reality in which they are placed. Evolution may explain how we have evolved to see holes, so as not to fall in them, or how to avoid dangerous snakes, so as not to be killed. It is, however, much harder to see how human reason can soar to the heights of understanding physical processes at the heart of the development of a universe that is so immense. Many turn to science, in the midst of such stress on diversity, as a unifying factor. It seems to show us truths about one world, when there is so much diversity of belief and disagreement. Yet what gives us the right to talk so glibly of one world? How did science arrive at that assumption?

We have already referred in passing to the polytheism of the ancient Greeks, and many societies have found it easy to assume the existence of many deities. They could even be in conflict with each other. That was what precisely aroused the scorn of Xenophanes. Yet the appeal to different deities was for many a way of explaining the mysteries and power of the physical world. Everything could be understood in terms of agency, on the model of human agency. As we shall see, it seems to be a feature of the human mind that we want to understand why things are as they are. Normally, human experience suggests that that is often the result of something that has been deliberately done by an agent. When the sea exhibits great power, or when the lightning flashes and the thunder rolls, or even when the leaves on the trees rustle, it seems natural to jump to the conclusion that someone is doing it. The earliest moves to recognisable physical theory had to involve a step away from an explanation in terms of personal agency. For the Greeks and Romans, the invocation of Poseidon, or Neptune, could explain the movements of the sea. Even the movement of trees could be seen in terms of what tree spirits, or 'dryads', were up to. When Thales and other early thinkers began to talk of impersonal but active entities such as water, air, fire and eventually atoms, the focus was moved from gods to matter, from the personal to the impersonal, even from purpose to cause. Modern scientific explanation cannot countenance final explanation in terms of personal agency, in the way that even Aristotle encouraged. 'The fairies at the bottom of the garden did it' is the antithesis of what is regarded as a rational explanation. Even so, why can there be such assurance that we all confront only one world and not a multitude of diverse ones? It seems impossible as a matter of logic to refer to a multitude of different worlds each hermetically sealed from the other, unless we imagine ourselves to be inhabiting the one world that includes them all. We have some-how to transcend them.

The early philosophers (or scientists) such as Thales, were looking for what we now term physical explanations. Above all, however they were 'monists' looking for one explanation. It was meant to be an explanation of the one world that confronts everyone. How far such early thinkers were explicitly denying any divinity, rather than asserting what we would now call pantheism, is probably an anachronistic question. Later atomists were sure that their physical explanations were a challenge to religion. Even so, the urge for the earliest thinkers in the Greek world was to a unitary explanation of everything. They were looking for the one reality behind many appearances. Parmenides, who influenced Plato, stressed the importance of 'the one that is'.[18] For him, what is was unitary, and its opposite, what is not, was just nothing. It was not anything. The idea behind this logical puzzle was that there is merely one reality, and this echoed through subsequent philosophy. One can even see in this the beginnings of a philosophical understanding of the one God behind all appearances. It is the harbinger of the contrast, that Plato embraced, between the transitory world of sights and sounds and the one, eternal, changeless world, the contrast between the many and the one.

Materialists have always been impatient with such duplication of realities, remaining content with the world we experience through our senses. Yet the basic conflict between the one and the many has haunted Western thought ever since. Is there one underlying unity somehow subsisting behind the undoubted plurality and diversity of human experience and belief? Is there one eternal, unchanging reality that lies apart from the many transitory events we experience

---

[18] Fr 2 in Kirk, Raven and Schofield

from day to day? Yet even this dispute about the one and the many, the eternal and the transitory, coalesces around the idea that we do all live in the same world. The question is its nature. Despite the blandishments of Protagoras, the foundations of both philosophy and science themselves rested on the notion of a single reality. Even disagreements about whether the physical world was composed ultimately of one substance in many guises, such as water, or an irreducible multitude of things, say earth, air, fire and water, were disagreements about the constituents of the one world.

There can also be disagreements between different forms of polytheism and monotheism. Is there one God or more? It is important to distinguish questions about numbers of divinities as part of the same reality, and the related idea that in fact different gods exist 'for' different religions or different places. The former question is a legitimate topic of disagreement in disputes between religions; The latter idea makes any dialogue between religions in principle impossible. Yet we cannot escape the fact that different religions are often explicitly at odds with each other. A good example is the rejection in the name of monotheism by Muslims of any claim of a final revelation through Jesus Christ. As one Muslim theologian puts it:[19] 'The Quran would dismiss such claims as Christian fanaticism, betraying an overly developed devotion to a mere messenger of God who made no claim to divinity or universality of mission'. Here we have a claim to understand the Christian message, and at the same time reject the idea that Christ is the divine Saviour as 'blasphemous mythology'.[20] Islam's severe monotheism forbids it to entertain ideas of God as 'three Persons in one Trinity'.

Disagreement and even quarrelling between different religions is not a consequence of monotheism alone. Polytheists could find other religions a threat too, as when the worshippers of Diana of Ephesus ganged up on St Paul, as narrated in the *Acts of the Apostles*. However, the fact that different gods could be revered in different places was not necessarily a problem. Polytheists could easily identify apparently different gods with each other, as happened with the Greek Poseidon and the Roman Neptune. Local gods and goddesses could similarly be seen as part of the Roman pantheon. A local Celtic goddess, Sulis, was worshipped in the Roman city of Aquae Sulis, now Bath, and was immediately identified with Minerva, the Roman goddess of wisdom. Minerva had been in turn identified with the Greek goddess Athene. All this spoke to a belief in one objective reality, which could be, and was, recognised in different places, though under different descriptions.

---

[19] S. Akhtar. *The New Testament in Muslim Eyes: Paul's Letter to the Galatians*, p. 132
[20] Akhtar, p. 89

A polytheistic system could easily embrace the worship of one more god or goddess. It could not accept there is only one God, so that the objects of its own worship did not exist. The monotheistic claim of one God and one reality inevitably makes claims to the same kind of universality. Yet this is far from being universally accepted. We return to the question why, if there is one God, are there so many different religions, and so many who are willing to dismiss all religion? Why, indeed, should such a God be apparently so willing to make it difficult for humans to believe in Him? These are issues to which we must now turn.

2 One God

2.1 One Creation

Perhaps the question of why God could allow so many kinds of religion can be turned round. We can wonder why, when there are beliefs in so many gods, or different ideas about the same God, we should believe not just in any particular religion, but in any one God. Why not follow the Romans and just make room for additional gods in the pantheon of deities? Why restrict oneself to the one God? Diversity is 'inclusive', it may seem. Opposing it smacks of the urge to dominate and exclude. The monotheistic stress on one God is a characteristic of Judaism, Christianity and Islam. Yet are they even worshipping the same God? Do they think they are? Much depends on how God is identified. If He is seen as the 'Father of our Lord Jesus Christ', we are already in distinctive Christian territory. If, though, what is in question is the nature and purpose of the physical universe, the identification of the one God as Creator may provide a platform on which all three Abrahamic faiths can join. Similarly reference to the 'God of Abraham' may find acceptance by all three.

The stress on diversity and divergence begins to take us away from the picture of one world confronting us all. We then give up on the yearning to see unity behind diversity, a reality behind appearance. Yet from the beginnings of Greek philosophy, we have seen how people have been impelled to look for a single explanation of everything. That was true even in a polytheistic world, where the gods seemed to provide little explanation for the existence of the world or its nature. They certainly did not give any guidance about how humans should live together.

Modern science, from the time of Newton, and the founding of the Royal Society in London in 1660, assumes the existence of one world that reason could investigate. That stemmed from a theistic belief in the one God who had created it. Their belief that one mind permeated the universe gave early scientists in the modern age the confidence to assume that there was one rational structure built into the nature of things, and that one Reason had produced it. The fact they believed that humans were made in the image of the one God also gave them assurance that human rationality had the capability of unlocking, at least in part, the secrets of the physical universe. This gave answers to the question of why the physical world should behave a uniform way and why should it be accessible to human rationality.

If there was not one God, no purpose, behind physical appearances, the idea of one common underlying reality would be very hard to uphold. When we all confront in the physical world of sights and sounds in all its complexity, difference, and even apparent confusion, why should anyone try to find a unified explanation? Science has to assume an ontological unity between the apparent diversity. Different sciences can have different perspectives on the nature of reality, so that, for instance, biology need not be dissolved into physics. Each can have its own integrity. Arguments can rage about how different sciences should be combined with each other. Unity and harmony need not demand the domination of one science over another or the reduction of all sciences to a basic physics. Diversity may itself be a fact of the one world, so that reality can be investigated in different ways. Yet just as biology can be complementary to physics, science can assume that different forms of knowledge about the one world can be pursued in a way that one gives illumination to another. A direct contradiction in science has to be a sign that our understanding is deficient. A single harmonious world need not be a simple one. Reality itself can be complex but itself still one.

Belief in one Creator can, and did, produce an assurance that we face one Creation. Current speculation in some parts of physics about the possibility of an infinite number of universes can leave ordinary scientific method far behind. Science can only deal with the reality it directly confronts and assume that all physical reality in our universe will operate according to the same principles. The idea of alien universes operating with utterly different laws, entertained by some speculative physicists, is in the strictest terms as metaphysical as any belief in a transcendent God. They are unverifiable by any current or possible science.[21] Whether they exist or can be made consistent with the idea of one God is a large question. The idea was put forward by scientists and mathematicians, in part, as a response to the so-called 'anthropic principle' in physics.[22] That ties the conditions necessary for the existence of human life to the initial conditions at the start of the universe. Any infinitesimal variation would have made life impossible. That could suggest one initial purpose, but the idea of all

---

[21] See R. Trigg, *Beyond Matter*, p. 42ff.   [22] Trigg, p. 42ff.

possibilities being actualised, which is what an infinite number of universes suggests, seems to conceive of chance and not purpose the fundamental guide.

Influential among the founders of the Royal Society were theologians and philosophers based in Cambridge, called the Cambridge Platonists.[23] Their oft-repeated phrase was that reason is the 'candle of the Lord'. That gave an explicit link between the God of creation and the reason of His creatures. Human reason could thus be relied on as a means of illuminating reality, albeit with the pale flickering light of a candle. Humans share, if very slightly, in the rationality (the *logos* according to St John's Gospel) that permeates the world.

That makes the idea of humans correlative with the idea of God. The so-called 'death of God', proclaimed by Nietzsche, has inevitably been accompanied by collapse in the belief in a single common humanity. Without one God, as the foundation of everything, all that seems to be left is diversity, including a diversity of different kinds of humans and a diversity of realities constructed by myriad beliefs. Without a belief in a single Creator, we have to discard the idea of any physical reality that operates with basic regularities that we can rely on. The prime motive for belief in any ontological unity has been removed. Pressures mount for the splintering of reality and towards an ultimate, irresolvable diversity.

Similarly, there is removed any idea of natural law in a moral sense, demonstrating the possible costs and benefits of different courses of action for human beings. There are no external constraints from nature, on the behaviour of human beings, as the idea of nature itself is as illusionary as the idea of humanity. Without the concept of one God, those of one reality, one human nature, or one reality, all become difficult to sustain. The atheist would have it that we live in a godless, disenchanted universe. Certainly, a strong motive for believing in any ontological unity, even universe operating on single principles, has been removed.

It is often been said that polytheism was superseded by monotheism. Once the search for a single explanation of the world seemed important, there was an inexorable tug towards the notion of one principle guiding everything. This is certainly true in the history of Western thought, as we look at the development from the worship of Greek gods, all made in the image of men and women, but behaving even worse. The idea of antagonistic deities may have provided for rollicking stories and myths. They neither provided moral exemplars, nor any explanation for 'the nature of things'. The latter was the title of a Latin treatise in by the Roman poet Lucretius, purveying an atomist, and atheist, philosophy. The use of the singular in talking of 'the nature' was significant. The urge to see

---

[23] See C. Taliaferro and A. Teply, *Cambridge Platonist Spirituality*

one structure in everything, and perhaps even one purpose, is, as we shall see in Section 4, seemingly part of the deep cognitive architecture of humans. That provides a motive for believing in a one God with intentions and purposes.

2.2 The Oneness of God

Yet must the one God be the only spiritual entity? There seems room in some religious thinking for angels, archangels and the whole panoply of heaven. Angels, or messengers, are usually regarded as mere agents of God and not alternative deities. What would become problematic is if there was more than one God in seeming competition with God as Creator. Talk of the Devil, or Satan, can sometimes make it look as if the universe is a moral battleground between two equal forces, Good and Evil. Some religions have seen the world in these terms, but that is not monotheism. A power struggle between two gods raises the question whether either is worthy of human worship. If the good God is not fully in control, and merely trying to do His best, how admirable would that be? A bungling God, even one with good intentions, is hardly going to be the highest object of admiration possible for humans.

The problem of evil is a perennial issue for a monotheism that posits the goodness of God. Yet evil is seen as such only as a result of monotheism. Evil is identified precisely because of its comparison with the perfect goodness believed to inhere in the Godhead. Parts of Creation seem to be at odds with the purposes of God. Evil is recognised as such, because of its comparison with the perfect goodness believed to inhere in the Godhead. We recognise it because we consider it alien to the way things ought to be. If we use the existence of apparent evil as an argument against the existence of any God, we have to accept that such 'evil' can no longer carry the moral weight required. Humans just happen not to like certain things. We have already removed the very possibility of the universe being freighted with any single moral meaning.

The doctrine of the Trinity remains a definite obstacle for many who wish to proclaim a pure monotheism. Unitarians, from the eighteenth century on, tried to preach a form of Christianity that does not involve issues about the divinity of Christ, or any juggling between three persons and one God. The formula that God is three and one, and one in three, can seem mysterious, if not incoherent. We have already commented on Islam's repugnance to any departure from strict monotheism. One Muslim commentator draws the distinction succinctly between the two monotheistic religions: 'While God is necessarily one, the Christian deity derives relationship with his human creation in a relationist and Trinitarian monotheism rather than in a unitary and judicial one'.[24] That

---

[24] Akhtar, p. 256

explains the Islamic stress on the importance of a rule-driven life, on divine law, and its distinction from the Christian distrust of 'the law' as an end in itself. Islam stresses obedience to rules, while Christians see faith more in terms of a personal encounter with God.

When Unitarians withdraw from traditional Christian doctrine, they find it difficult to formulate a message distinctive from well-meaning secularism. Its aspirations to universality erode any specific content for its beliefs. However puzzling the doctrine of the Trinity might be to formulate, the denial of any part of it can be fatal to Christian faith. A belief in God the Father alone can easily result in the kind of deism popular in the eighteenth century, according to which God was seen the divine watchmaker who wound up the clockwork, but was unconcerned with what subsequently happens. Yet why should I worship a God totally unconcerned with me? Similarly, the denial of the divinity of Christ by a 'rational' theism removes the central claim of Christianity, that Jesus revealed God in a unique way. For Christians, the person of Jesus sums up what God means by humanity, and conversely what humans mean by God. As we shall see, an epistemological bridge between God and us is crucial in any attempt to gain knowledge of a transcendent God. Once Jesus is seen as a mere prophet, His role as a revelation of God wanes.

Similarly, denying the divinity of the Holy Spirit, the third person of the Trinity, immediately takes us back to a deism denying the agency of God in the world. God must be immanent as well as transcendent. He is present with us, as well as separate from us. Different branches of Christian thought can stress different persons of the Trinity. There is a diversity within Christianity, and Christian worship. Some would stress the glory of Almighty God our Creator, and others would value the relationship of Jesus, their brother, who suffered as we do. Others would, in a charismatic manner, look for the obvious workings of the Holy Spirit. Yet Christianity is always in trouble if it does not recognise the single Godhead in all its facets. The unity has to be apparent through diversity, with each person of the Trinity reflecting the nature of the whole. Christianity, as a religion, can become unbalanced in unpredictable ways if the three persons are not seen as one, or if one of the three is stressed to the exclusion of the others.

Even in the Old Testament, the Hebrew Bible, a strict monotheism was not always apparent. The Lord Jehovah at times has been made to appear simply 'the greatest of all gods', perhaps even a tribal God more powerful than rivals. Yet the very idea of God as Creator, with which Genesis begins, leaves no room for other competing gods. As the Psalmist says, 'the gods of the nations are idols of silver and gold, fashioned by human hands'.[25]

---

[25] Psalm 135

2.3 The Properties of God

The worlds of 'Athens' and 'Jerusalem' are sometimes distinguished in an attempt to distinguish the God of the philosophers and the God as shown in forms of revelation. Reason is somehow to be distinguished from our response to revelation. Yet once we genuinely see the need for worship, we should see that the object of worship must be genuinely worthy of that worship. That immediately stimulates the urge to understand better the object of our worship. Our reason, which for a theist, is a gift of God, has to be brought into play. To have faith, we must use our reason to grasp who, or what, we are putting our faith in. For instance, if God is not in control of things, He is not omnipotent. The idea of one God and the idea of omnipotence are deeply entwined. The existence of more than one God as a rational possibility seems a contradiction. Different gods may have super-human powers, but they are super-humans, not the ultimate explanation for everything. The urge to find some unifying principle still remains. That is why the Greek gods proved so inadequate as explanations for serious thinkers about the underlying nature of things. Whilst it is tempting, and, as we shall see, even possibly natural, to see events in terms of personal agency, explaining multiple events in terms of multiple agencies merely pushes a search for understanding back a stage. The urge to find some unifying principle still remains, and a theistic explanation sees that principle in personal terms with talk of meaning and purpose. Materialist or physical explanations, on the other hand, see things in terms of causation, and impersonal forces.

As with omnipotence, all the properties attributed to the one God deny any possibility of God being limited. God's infinity tells that He is not bounded or constrained by anything. Because, for example, He is regarded as omniscient, His knowledge cannot be confined to the limits of one place or time. He is present anywhere. Many philosophers have concluded over the centuries that God's eternity cannot consist in mere everlasting time, but somehow be beyond any spatiotemporal framework. We cannot limit God by placing Him somewhere, or at one time. He does not find it difficult to see into the future or remember the past, precisely because He is not located in the present. We shall later see that the idea of someone knowing everything is not as alien to human understanding as one might first imagine.

The fact that no one can hide from God, or deceive Him, must be crucial to any religious understanding. God sees everything and knows everything. Polytheists might hope to propitiate whichever god they prefer to worship, whether the god or goddess of the city, or of their trade. Yet the one God who knows everything would seem less likely to be manipulated, and more demanding of proper behaviour. We are all familiar with the fact that people, and not just children, can behave very differently once they think no one is watching. People do not just fear being caught. They can be ashamed to be seen doing certain things. Empirical studies have shown how even a face drawn on a wall is sometimes sufficient to deter children from stealing sweets that are available in a room.

If God is literally thought to be watching us, our behaviour will be affected, particularly, if we believe that, as a result, we are liable to be punished. Evolutionary biology has shown that belief in supernatural punishment is itself a highly adaptive belief, promoting Darwinian fitness. It can encourage cooperative behaviour. One writer talks of the wide prevalence of beliefs in supernatural punishment. He claims that 'negative supernatural consequences are common to religions across the world's cultures, and throughout history'.[26] Belief in multifarious gods or spirits with limited power is never going to be as effective as a belief in a God who sees everything, since there is no escape from such a God.

There may be evolutionary reasons favouring such beliefs, but the drive to monotheism has a rational basis. Quarrelling and competing gods do not provide a moral example, nor do they seem able to provide a coherent explanatory basis. They lack the power, and the knowledge, that can inspire awe and worship. Some will immediately object that obedience to God on the basis of His power and knowledge is simply the worship of power, or the result of a grovelling fear. What kind of God would we then be worshipping? Even if there is a single principle at work in the world, is it good, bad or morally neutral? Does it care for humans or is it indifferent to their fate? These are substantive questions, and reason may not be able to provide complete answers. If we try to argue from the nature of the world to God, we may see rationality and order in the world and see that is indicative of a divine mind. We might even be inclined to see purpose in the development of the universe. The world, however, may still seem morally ambivalent, and if there is a Creator, we may be none the wiser of its, or His, nature.

An omniscient and omnipotent God cannot have competitors. Similarly, two separate omniscient gods could not have separate purposes unknown to each other. Yet if their purposes were fully known to each other, it is unclear how separate the two gods would truly be. Once the idea of omnipresence is added to the ingredients, it seems impossible for two separate gods to be equally omnipresent. They would have to be identical, as the traditional notion of the 'identity of indiscernibles' makes clear. Philosophers have often dubbed God

---

[26] D. Johnson, *God is Watching You*, p. 57

as 'the greatest possible being, something than which nothing greater can be conceived'. This was the basis of Anselm's controversial ontological argument for the existence of God. As long as there are two gods, it is always possible to imagine that one could have more power than the other, or more of whatever property is in question. In any conception of God, therefore, we have to be driven remorselessly to the notion of one God. As long as there are several gods, one could always be conceived of as in some sense greater than the rest.

A corollary of the idea of unity, is that of universality. Even if there were other spiritual entities, they would be creatures of God and not alternative deities. Oneness, singularity, cannot make room for diversity. There can only be one Creator. Anyone who says 'may your God go with you' may sound very open-minded, but the words reveal deep confusion about the nature of any deity. There is simply no room for different gods, whatever the diversity of religious understanding that exists. Ontology cannot be discarded, but is a vital guiding principle, which gives point to our search for knowledge. Human abilities are limited and unlikely to get to grips with the whole of the nature of reality. Within theology, it is clear that finite minds are going to struggle to gain glimmerings of the nature of that which by definition is infinite.

Sometimes the success of present-day science blinds us to the limits of scientific understanding. Some may object to the comparison of theology and science by pointing out that theology is invoking a different kind of world than the world which we know we inhabit. It seems to refer to a different realm, or level, of reality, the existence of which would be denied by many. This objection points to a fear of metaphysics that has haunted much contemporary philosophy.[27] Yet science itself is stretching further and further beyond what is directly accessible to human beings. Theory becomes ever more distant from immediate observation. Whatever the context, the fundamental distinction between reality and human knowledge of it must remain, and the limitations on human beings must be recognised.

2.4 Pluralism in Religion

Might different religions be simply focusing on different aspects of the same reality? There is a well-worn Indian tale of blind men feeling different parts of the same elephant, and coming to different conclusions about its one nature. Certainly this brings out the consequences of limitations on our knowledge. It shows how we can all have different perceptions and perspectives of the same thing, just as climbers can climb the same mountain from different sides.

---

[27] See R. Trigg, *Beyond Matter*

Perhaps this could enable us to come to the comforting conclusion that we are all in some sense right because of our partial knowledge.

This kind of insight was developed in a classic book by the philosopher of religion, John Hick. In championing what he termed 'the Real', he tried to hold together the undoubted fact of different religions, and their different understandings of the divine, with a strong philosophical realism. He tried to combine undoubted religious differences and the idea of one objective reality. He thought that all beliefs have as their object of reference the same reality, even if they come to very different conclusions. He was trying to put forward a view that made what he termed 'post-axial' faiths equally respected. The faiths that he concentrated on stress the importance of salvation, through transforming human existence from being centred on self to being centred on Reality (with a capital letter).[28] This made his task much easier because he concentrated on world religions such as the Abrahamic faiths, Buddhism and Hinduism. In widening the sphere for toleration and inclusiveness, he still refused to engage with other religions which might not have the kind of ethical content that might appeal to a Christian philosopher of religion like himself. Some religions involve devil worship, human sacrifice and other horrors. Even though he wanted to be open to other religions by underplaying the doctrinal content of particular religions, his inclusiveness had its limits. Monotheism was watered down into a vague gesture towards 'the Real', but it still could not include everything, if it was to have any content at all.

Hick's intention is to hold a monotheism that still recognises the many images of ultimate reality that occur in world religions. For him, the Real is 'present to all forms of existence as the ground of their ever-changing being'.[29] That is the ontological basis for religion, but our understanding of this will be culturally conditioned and vary from religion to religion. What we think of as the Real is mediated by what Hick curiously calls 'the gods of the great monotheistic faiths', which are all simultaneously manifestations of the Real.[30] He quotes with approval an Eastern saying that 'the Real is one, though sages name it variously'.[31]

This theological approach is attractive to those of a liberal disposition who hesitate to suggest their own faith is superior to that of other religions, at least the respectable ones. We all in our own way have different visions of whatever the Real is. So-called pluralism in religion is embraced, though within limits. Yet at this point the vacuity of the position becomes apparent. Hick is consciously following Kant's basic epistemology, which stresses the role of the

---

[28] See J. Hick, *An Interpretation of Religion*, e.g. p. 33   [29] Hick, p. 252   [30] Hick, p. 272
[31] Hick, p. 253

formation of the human mind in the formation of concepts. Kant was looking at rational agents as such, and had no truck with alternative conceptual schemes. Even so, his main point was the differentiation between reality as it is it is in itself, and the world as it appears to us. That is his distinction between *noumena* and *phenomena*. Hick's starting point, however, is not human rationality but different religions which see reality in different ways. These different perspectives are described by Hick as different 'personae', whether the Christian Trinity, Shiva, Allah, Vishnu or whoever.[32] This is meant to embody a pluralism that is not relativist, since it is focused on one reality. Yet Kant's epistemology always made reality a mere regulative concept emptied of all content. It could easily be later discarded by philosophers as a wheel that was not turning anything else. The idea of inaccessible 'things-in-themselves' could seem redundant.

In the specific case of religion, if all our understandings are on the epistemological side, the 'Real' becomes so nebulous as to drop out of sight as irrelevant. We can never engage with anything more than a culturally conditioned idea. This has serious consequences. Asserting that we are never in a position to break out of our cocoons and see the true nature of things is ultimately to undermine all religion. We may merely be projecting our understanding on to nothing, as thinkers such as Feuerbach have alleged. If the Real is merely 'the noumenal ground of the encountered gods and experienced absolutes witnessed to by the religious traditions', we can say nothing definite about it.[33] Hick says bluntly of the Real in itself that 'it cannot be said to be one or many, person or thing, substance or process, good or evil, purposive or non-purposive'.[34]

This conclusion is disastrous even for monotheism as a regulative idea. Hick has admitted that such monotheism is itself a cultural construct, because we cannot see beyond the veil created by whichever conceptual scheme we have adopted. He is himself concerned with the question why we should 'use the term "Real" in the singular'.[35] He wants to affirm the true ultimacy of 'the Real' but admits that 'it cannot literally be numbered'.[36] Nothing could illustrate better the collapse of Hick's realism and monotheism into vacuity. The pluralism that aims at a total inaccessible reality will collapse into something surprisingly like relativism. A monotheism that cannot even proclaim the oneness of God immediately contradicts itself. The admission that we cannot even be sure that the universe contains purpose or is ultimately good, let alone that the root of all things is personal, undermines the foundations of monotheism.

---

[32] Hick, p. 244   [33] Hick, p. 241   [34] Hick, p. 246   [35] Hick, p. 248   [36] Hick, p. 249

Hick may think that there cannot be a plurality of ultimates, but it leaves us wondering how his philosophical framework allows for the truth of any particular religion. In his desire to espouse a pluralism that recognises the good in all religions, or at least the ones he chooses to sympathise with, he removes any good reason for believing in any of them. Given that his vision of ultimate reality is something so ineffable that it is neither singular or plural, a reverential silence seems the only possibility. How is something, we know not what, so very different from nothing? Perhaps the silence of a Quaker meeting would be the only possible form of worship.

Hick himself set great store by the stress that what he terms 'the great traditions' place on ethical characteristics, such as the love and compassion 'epitomised by the Golden Rule'.[37] Yet what is the connection between religious beliefs and morality? The idea that we could discover a basis for ethics in the convergence of different beliefs is optimistic. Without a strong metaphysical basis as a uniting force, we are left with different understandings of human life within religion and outside it. The notion of human nature as a unitary phenomenon is itself normally the product of a belief in a God who created us all. It is no coincidence that, as has been mentioned, the retreat of monotheistic belief has led to the collapse of the assumption that 'humanity' is a universal notion. We are just left with different beliefs about what is beneficial and harmful to human beings who themselves differ radically. Any conception of a morality that can make universal claims becomes illusory. We can no longer hope that morality can be seen as essentially following from the guidance of a God who knows what is good for us. We no longer have to be responsible to the one God. Without a single human nature, we cannot appeal to any basic human needs or interests. Even the Golden Rule itself, as upheld by Hick, becomes meaningless. We cannot treat others as we would wish ourselves to be treated, if the others cannot be assumed to be like us in important respects.

Once the 'Real', whatever it may be, becomes remote, the connection between its nature and our behaviour becomes tenuous. Monotheism requires a closer relationship. Moral progress depends on an idea of purposive development towards an ideal. If there is no standard of goodness beyond the agreement of some current consensus, whether religious or not, there can be no possibility of aiming at anything good beyond ourselves, let alone of being under judgement for not attempting to reach it. It is a commonplace in contemporary society that equality matters and that all humans are of equal importance. Yet it is often not made clear why this should be. Why should I sacrifice my interests to those of others? It is a distinctively monotheistic tenet that all are equal in the sight of

---

[37] Hick, p. 316

the Creator, and that we are all brothers, and sisters, because we have the same Father. The 'brotherhood of man' is an old-fashioned phrase now, but clearly resonates with an implied reference to the monotheistic background that produced it.

Without God as a unifying factor, diversity becomes the ultimate fact, both between societies and also increasingly within them. Notions of the common good collapse into the idea of different personal 'values', which may be at odds with each other. There is no ideal state of affairs, and no notion of how humans should behave. There is no one unified divine will, which is engaged with the world, creating order and regularity within it, so that we can anticipate the consequences of our actions. The idea of ultimate responsibility to God, or to anything, disappears. Human life becomes purposeless and the idea of moral progress becomes unintelligible. Morality has to be either purely subjective, or, at most, a matter of local convention varying from place to place. Without monotheism, it cannot be grounded in the way things are, or the way humans are meant to be. There is a close link between the idea of the one God and one morality, just as there is between one God and one humanity.

3 The Otherness of God

3.1 God and Diversity

The idea of one God seems difficult to reconcile with a genuine diversity of religious belief and practice. Yet there is great diversity, and always has been. Given monotheism, how is it that everything splinters so catastrophically? The idea of unity amongst all that diversity seems baffling. Given that there are many religions, with diverse views about what ultimately exists, what grounds are there for believing in one God in the first place? Why should one religion, or a narrow group of them, be right and the rest wrong? Could any be right? It is easy to dismiss those who disagree with us as mistaken, but they say the same about our views. Why should we believe in one God, given many religions? We have seen how the answer must lie in the need to provide a single rational explanation for all things. Even if we say that *the* ultimate reality about *the* world is its ultimate diversity, we are still looking to the idea of one truth holding universally. Once one posits supernatural entities, one is further remorselessly led along a path to an idea of one controlling principle or rationale. An explanation in terms of persons leads us towards an idea of one God. The pluralism of alternative explanations seems, in the end, to provide little or no explanation at all.

We are entitled to ask why diversity of religious belief persists, if it does not ultimately reflect the nature of things. A scientific explanation that leaves us with conflicting scientific theories shows that we have still not fully understood the workings of the one world. In fundamental physics, the theory of general relativity cannot be properly reconciled with quantum physics. There is as yet no agreed, self-consistent theory of quantum gravity. Although physicists have to make the best of this, our understanding is still limited. The current scientific approach is not to give a metaphorical shrug of one's shoulders and celebrate the diversity of scientific theories. Something is not right. Our knowledge is deficient. Physics deals with both the very great and the very small. Yet both the furthest reaches of the universe and the most microscopic of subatomic particles lie outside the reach even of modern technology. We are finite beings limited by our position in time and space. The same dynamic arises with religious claims about the nature of reality. If, by definition, finite minds encounter the infinite, and spatiotemporal beings reach out to what is alleged to be outside time and space, human limitations become more apparent. It may not be surprising that differences remain amongst humans about what lies beyond.

Yet is not religion, with its demands for personal commitment,[38], very different from a mere disinterested search for scientific truth? Faith, it will be claimed, is not a mere rational weighing of alternatives, but demands a way of life with definite moral demands. This ignores the fact, already referred to, that faith cannot ultimately be separated from a rational description of the object of our trust or worship. If religions are not to be understood as explaining the nature of the world or the place of humanity in it, religious diversity simply becomes a political problem and not a philosophical one. It becomes a matter of how we can live together, and not a question of who is right. There is, it seems, nothing to be right about. If religions are mere patterns of life without any aspirations to metaphysical claims, questions of polytheism versus monotheism, and monotheism versus atheism, simply fall to the ground. Agnosticism, covering those who 'do not know' about religion, is also ruled out, since there is nothing to have knowledge about. Some ways of life might seem preferable to others, but that would be merely a matter of individual inclination. The question of truth drops out.

The monotheistic claim is that behind everything, the 'ground of our being' is a single form of reality which we call God. Yet, as we saw with the work of John Hick, talking of 'Reality' does not take us very far. The monotheistic religions see God in personal terms. The three Abrahamic religions share a similar vision of God as Creator. Judaism and Islam particularly see Him as the ultimate giver of law, showing us how we should live. Ethical qualities such as justice and mercy are also attributed to Him.

---

[38] See R. Trigg, *Reason and Commitment*

The fact that God is seen in such personal terms explains why He cannot be referred as 'it'. It is inadequate, though, to see God as male, or female. Both terms can carry with them unwanted implications, but unlike in, say Finnish, it is not possible in English to refer to persons but not attribute gender. Referring to 'God' as 'She' can invoke traditional connections seen in pagan religions between divinity and fertility. Interestingly, the Greek for the Holy Spirit, *pneuma*, is a neuter (non-gendered) term, and 'it' can be understood as an impersonal force, though even that idea sits uncomfortably with the doctrine of 'three persons in one'.

This points to the 'otherness' of God. Seeing God in our own image belittles the idea of the Creator, before whom, it is said we can only bow down and worship. That is an idea less easy to grasp in a democratic age, when monarchs are expected to be ordinary people like us. It is far from the mystique of eastern potentates, before whom their subjects prostrated themselves in worship, literally lying down face forward on the ground in front of them. Significantly, this is precisely what the ' Wise Men' are recounted as doing before the baby Jesus in Bethlehem.

Modern theologians stress the love of God towards us, sometimes down-playing His sheer difference from us and His intrinsic majesty. Like modern monarchs, God is expected to be accessible and approachable. There is a tug between ideas of God's utter difference and otherness, and our own need to relate to Him. If God is formed in our own image, He is by definition like us. Once we begin to stress His transcendence, words become inadequate. The Greeks, of whom Xenophanes was so contemptuous, did not have this trouble. Their gods were mere extensions of themselves.

The question remains not just why in the face of the one reality there are so many diverse views, but also, why, if there is a God, it seems so difficult for humans to understand what He is like. Why does not God to make it easier to believe in Him? The mere fact of diversity of belief reflects the difficulty that reasonable people have in coming to any clear belief about God and His nature. As we have mentioned, it can itself provide an obstacle to belief. As Robert McKim suggests: 'Religious ambiguity . . . enables us to see it is understandable that outsiders disagree with us'.[39] Religious diversity is undoubtedly an out-come of the interpretation of complex phenomena. That, though, hardly helps the question, if there is a God, why He has not made Himself better known to us?

3.2 God's 'Hiddenness'

Perhaps God has shown Himself, and those who refuse to acknowledge this are culpable. Yet many, honestly seeking truth, still find the reality of God hard to

---

[39] R. McKim, *Religious Diversity and Religious Progress*, p. 8

grasp. It is in this context that the so-called hiddenness argument has been produced, notably by J. L. Schellenberg.[40] It is explicitly targeted at the paradox of a personal God who cares for us, but apparently makes it so difficult to enter into a personal relationship with Him. Schellenberg assumes that a God of perfect love would be open to a 'meaningful conscious relationship' with us and 'will ensure that we always are in a position to participate in it'.[41] For Schellenberg, the fact that many people, throughout history, have not been able to believe, is a knockdown argument against the existence of a loving God, open to personal relationships. Schellenberg does not argue against the idea of some ultimate standard of truth, but dismisses deism.[42] He says: 'Deism's creator doesn't care enough about us to play any religious role'.

The issue for Schellenberg is not whether there is an ultimate reality, even some distant Creator, but whether there is a personal God of love who wants to be in a relationship with us. The thought behind all this is that if the evidence for God is inconclusive, that itself 'should be taken as a conclusive reason for disbelief'.[43] His argument is that if there were a God, as a loving heavenly Father, He could never allow the evidence to be inconclusive. Agnosticism has to lead to atheism. It is significant that Schellenberg talks of love and personal relationships, but refers to reason and evidence, and presents his argument in logically deductive form. Love and dispassionate reasoning are not always easily combined. What then is the nature of the love being invoked, both on the part of God towards humans and humans to God?

Some revelation of God has to be at the root of all religion. A remote, and inaccessible God becomes irrelevant to human projects and capacities. The nature of such a God would make all religion pointless. We would be trying to engage with a 'something we know not what', and, in the end, that seems indistinguishable from nothing. God cannot be so wholly other that we cannot say anything about the divine nature. Language may be inadequate, but if it cannot be employed at all, religion must be emptied of any content. If we make God like ourselves, that does not make Him divine enough, but making Him utterly transcendent reduces us to silence.

Schellenberg's challenge that God should make Himself better known to us assumes we would be sure of God's proper nature. We could simply talk of God's love with the assumptions of human love. Arguments drawing analogies from human to divine love to God's love always failed to answer the question how comparison of the known with an unknown grounds our knowledge of the

---

[40] See Schellenberg, *The Hiddenness Argument.*   [41] Schellenberg, p. 60.
[42] Scellenberg, p. 18.   [43] Schellenberg, p. 21

latter. It projects what we are familiar with on something that seems inaccessible.

Why should we expect divine love to be expressed in the same way as human love? Why should a loving God wish this love to be expressed in a personal relationship which is satisfying for the believer? Schellenberg is producing a philosophical argument, depending on reason and logic, rather than on any alleged revelation. He assumes that any God, 'greater than which cannot be conceived' must have the attributes of perfect love, and perfect goodness. In this, he explicitly goes beyond any deistic claim about the existence of a Creator as the origin of things. He is making an assumption about what the nature of that Creator has to be. Yet, given great religious diversity in world religions over the years, it is unclear why we should assume so easily that God is good, or God is love, in the same way that humans might aspire to goodness or to be loving.

Even if there is some divinity as the Source of all things, why should it be concerned for our interests? An Australian philosopher, Tim Mulgan, argues that although there is a God, with a purpose, we have no good reason to believe that human beings are an essential part of God's plan for the cosmos, or are metaphysically special. There could be other beings superior to ourselves. He proceeds on the assumption that somewhere in the universe there is a value greater than anything found in human life'.[44] He explicitly dismisses revelation and his argument is that 'God does not love individual human beings; that God has no interest in the fate of humanity, and the presence of human beings is a cosmic accident'. His argument is summed up pithily in the assertion that 'while it is about *something*, the universe is not about *us*'.

This is reminiscent of the deism that leads to atheism. A God who has no concern for us can easily be ignored. This was the path taken in the eighteenth century, with rational arguments that repudiated specific revelation. The argument shows that it is possible to conceive of one God, the designer of the universe or multi-verse, without imagining that humanity has to have any role in God's purposes. Anyone who is impressed with the intrinsic order of the universe, and wonders why it is expressible in mathematical form, with an inherent rationality, may accept that the positing of a designer mind may seem an explanation. Whether it was a mind that paid particular attention to humans will be open to question, and Mulgan asks that. There may seem little reason why we would think humans were of particular importance.

God may not be limited, but the world may still seem morally ambiguous. Saying that God is good by definition makes it opaque as to what is meant. One could take the alternative stance and deny that goodness is an attribute of God at

---

[44] T. Mulgan, *Purpose in the Universe*, p. 219

all. Why should the Creator be good in a sense we recognise, caring for the fate of individual humans? Schellenberg's assumption is that God is open to personal relationships with humans. It is understandable why humans would like to think that they can be loved by God, but what guarantee is there that it is so?

Conceiving God in familiar terms does not take account of the transcendence of God. Although we may think that the universe must have a single purpose, and be created for a reason, there has to be a limit as to how far we can discover the character of the Creator merely by definition. The search for a purpose can lead us to the idea of one point of origin, one centre of power and knowledge. Reason may well allow us to conclude there cannot be multiple gods. We are left with the question whether pure reason, and an appeal to metaphysical necessity, can conclude that God is perfectly loving and good. Is the universe despite appearances, benevolent? Have we any right to some form of cosmic optimism that all will be well?

A feature of God's otherness is His difference from Creation. Theism is not pantheism. God's immanence cannot be stressed to the detriment of the idea of transcendence. This implies the total distinctness of God from any forms of human understanding. He is metaphysically 'self-subsistent'. God's transcendence entails metaphysical realism. Divine reality is wholly other and separate from human understanding. The idea that God could be a projection of human minds must always be a profoundly atheist one. Even so, philosophers sympathetic to religion have been be prone to anti-realist interpretations that see religions as expressions of ways of life, perhaps inspired by particular stories, rather than claims to truth. Currents in twentieth-century philosophy led some to repudiate any appeal to metaphysics, even in a way that must undermine all religion.[45]

God's independent reality creates a chasm between divinity and humans that can easily encourage scepticism. Yet God's otherness entails that we should not easily assume that He has any particular characteristics other than formal logical ones associated with the logical demand that God is not limited. The philosophers' God may be worthy of worship in some respects, but seems remote from the God proclaimed by revealed religions, such as Christianity. God's utter distinctness entails a dualism of worlds, the spiritual reality inhabited by God, and the fragile, spatiotemporal, physical one, with which we are familiar.

3.3 Athens and Jerusalem

Dualism creates difficulties for those who see the world in monistic, usually materialist, terms. Many find the idea of different kinds of reality, or levels of

---

[45] See R. Trigg, *Reason and Commitment*; *Reality at Risk: A Defence of Realism in Philosophy and the Sciences*, 2nd ed.; *Beyond Matter: Why Science Needs Metaphysics*

reality, anathema. Even if everything cannot be within the reach of actual or possible science, God's otherness continues to pose the question of how we can understand what appears to be unknowable. In particular, even if we have certain expectations about human love, are we justified in extending those to God? Should God behave as we think He ought? If, to echo Isaiah, God's ways are not our ways and His thoughts are not our thoughts,[46] how are we to know God's care would be manifested for us? It seems wrong to suggest that God should simply behave as we think He ought. As Michael Rea comments in response to the hiddenness argument: 'Divine transcendence implies *humility about expectations*', and *humility about expectations* implies that violated expectations on divine love and goodness do not support claims like "no perfectly loving God exists".[47] The idea of God must imply that He is not a mere reflection of our desires. The distinction between the transcendent God of monotheism and the squabbling gods of the Greek pantheon poses the large question of how He could be manifested to human beings.

The philosophers' God and the worshippers' God can seem in opposition. Sometimes characterised as a battle between Athens and Jerusalem, between perhaps reason and revelation, the different understandings of God sometimes seem far apart. Yet, if sense is to be made of monotheism, they have to coalesce. Love seems to imply vulnerability, the ability to sympathise, to suffer with the object of love. Yet the philosophers' God is by definition without suffering. He is changeless, impervious to alterations and circumstances, and unaffected by changes in the future. A loving God may be vulnerable, but, because of that, hardly seems to be worthy of awe and worship. Moreover, love seems to imply an involvement in human affairs that implies duration. For philosophers, God has traditionally been outside time and space in a realm of changeless eternity. Aristotle's 'unmoved mover' is an example of a God who cannot make Himself vulnerable. Once God's otherness is qualified, so that we concentrate on a God within us and among us, His accessibility has increased but His majesty is compromised. If God suffers like us, how can there be any hope beyond suffering? God's transcendence cannot be compromised, without His power and glory being put into question.

Reason and revelation have often been thought to be in tension with each other. The Christian theologian, Karl Barth, thought that no one could think of, or conceive of, God apart from revelation. He argued that God 'is known only to Himself'.[48] Barth was, for this reason, critical of natural theology as a project, which tries to see traces of God in the natural world and argues from the world to

---

[46] Isaiah, 55, 8–9   [47] M. Rea, *The Hiddenness of God*, p. 57
[48] K. Barth, *Church Dogmatics*, Vol. 2, Part I, p. 197

God. Some would still see that as a form of general revelation, but Barth's stress was on the role of particular revelation, especially through the Bible. That is our only path to God, he thought. This approach, however, can encourage a damaging split between the ideas of faith and reason. 'Special' revelation would include God speaking through prophets, a holy book such as the Quran, or more specifically, in the case of Christianity, the person of Christ. Yet once we restrict the idea of revelation to particular episodes, and, in Barth's case, those of Christian revelation, the idea of a general monotheism collapses. If we can know nothing of God except through particular revelation, there can be no shared ground on which different religions might stand, particularly when the authenticity of a particular revelation is questioned.

This problem can be put most trenchantly by the question whether different monotheistic religions even worship the same God. That is not just a question of intellectual speculation, as it carries implications for how different religions, and even different branches of what is apparently the same religion, can approach each other. We may be more distrustful of those who do not worship the same God we do. Monotheists should agree that their common object of worship is the Creator of the universe, who would at least have the formal characteristics connected with the idea of infinity. Yet that does not explain why human minds envisage any supernatural reality, since it is by definition different from that of our familiar, natural world.

In the eighteenth century, the distinction between 'natural religion' and 'revealed religion' was stressed. Barth concentrated on the latter but that has the major disadvantage of ignoring the role of human rationality, as something common to all humans of all religions and cultures. Without some notion of reason and natural religion, different religions will always be divided up into different self-contained compartments with their own commitments allegedly derived from different revelations. They would not be able to agree on anything, since they could not appeal to any common source. 'Natural religion', however understood, should not be so easily discarded. In the face of competing and sometimes contradictory revelations, the basic question is what it purports to be about. Unless, as humans, we have some prior understanding of divinity, why should any experience, or event, be assumed to have a divine origin?

There could not be any divine revelation to minds that were not at least in part prepared to recognise it for what it was. Unless there is 'a God-shaped hole' in our understanding that such new knowledge could fit, how could any revelation get a grip on human life? God's transcendence may appear to have created an unbridgeable gulf between ourselves and God. For that reason, we may by nature have been prepared to understand our need for something divine. Perhaps humans are naturally prone to think in religious terms. Human minds are not blank slates on which anything can be written. This is to be pursued in the next Section.

3.4 Epistemic Distance

The alleged hiddenness of God shows that God cannot be so removed from us as to be irrelevant. The question is how such a gulf can be crossed. What bridges could there be to enable us to achieve knowledge of what may appear unknowable? There is a logical need for revelation of the divine in intelligible terms that humans can understand, if the divine is to have any purchase in human life. A similar conundrum arose for Plato when he posited his metaphysical system of 'Forms' as ideal patterns or standards, which are reflected only imperfectly in our world. He was insistent in his arguments against the relativists of his time that there were in reality such objective standards. Goodness was, he thought, an ultimate reality which could not be reduced to mere human thought or practice. Once that metaphysical reality was detached from the familiar physical one, how could we know the Forms? Plato's answer was that we had encountered their reality before our present lives, and can recollect it, given a proper process of education. Because our knowledge of the Forms was innate, it could be partially recovered.

Plato's metaphysical system has influenced Christian theology, from St Paul onwards. That is not enough to argue in its favour. A close comparison of the Forms and the God of monotheism can be questioned. The point is that philosophical difficulties arise when what there is (expressed in ontology), and how we can know it (as seen by epistemology), seem too far apart. Without a basic ontology, there is nothing beyond disparate human constructions of what purports to be knowledge but never can be. The different religions will then be seen as being about nothing, because nothing exists outside different systems of belief. Such scepticism, once accepted, can soon undermine our own will to believe what we do. We realise that we only think that something is true, but it never can be.

We might, as we shall see, have been born with innate dispositions to believe in the divine, or at least to comprehend something about its nature. Yet all religions, and in particular the monotheistic ones, have to rely on more than that. The Abrahamic religions accept that God has revealed Himself in particular ways at particular times through special people such as prophets, or, in the case of Christianity, even His own Son. In claiming that anyone who had seen Him had seen the Father, Jesus seemed to be claiming what God was like in terms that humans could comprehend.[49] There would, indeed, be no need for such

---

[49] St John, 14, 9

special revelation, if God had not, to some extent, been beyond our gaze. The very existence of the revealed religions, pointing to specific acts of divine revelation, assumes, from a philosophical point of view, that humans needed to be presented with such knowledge in a down-to-earth manner.

Even given the need for further revelation, we face the reality of apparent revelations which contradict each other. Jesus' identity with the Father, as proclaimed by Christianity, is an affront to monotheism, says Islam. Can such matters be resolved given any revelation of God's nature can only be partial? Even if we might attain perfect knowledge of God after this life, our finite nature restricts the possibility of our knowing in full now. St Paul's way of putting this is his Platonic contrast between looking at the reflection of a mirror and seeing face to face.[50] The mirrors of the ancient world were not glass ones giving a crystal-clear image. Made of highly polished metal, they could only produce a blurred reflection. Like the illumination of a flickering candle flame, in the image of reason as the candle of the Lord, the object of purported knowledge would be indistinct, and something of a riddle. Indeed St Paul uses the Greek word 'enigma' to describe the experience.

We must still ask why God would leave us so uncertain. Humans crave certainty, and religions tend to preach certainty. Who wants to devote their life to something that is unfocused and uncertain? As one Muslim writer has put it, 'No faith or ideology was ever founded on doubt or acknowledgement of diversity ... Certainty is a form of authority. It is intolerant of alternatives. In temperament, it is totalitarian, the temper of every successful protest and revolutionary movement'.[51]

This is a challenge to all religions, and particularly to monotheism, as we shall see in Section 5. If knowledge is partial, should not this make us hesitant in our faith, less willing and able to espouse it wholeheartedly? Authoritative claims to truth do seem to demand the certainty that can appear to validate commitment. Yet the very otherness of God could undermine our right to be sure of religious beliefs. One philosopher of religion put it this way:[52]

> When there is disagreement of the sort we find among the religious traditions, parties to the disagreement ought to hold the relevant beliefs tentatively, where this involves a recognition that you may be mistaken, or willingness to revise your beliefs, an openness to alternative beliefs, and an awareness that some of the competing beliefs may be plausible or even correct.

The mere existence of different religions, in the face of the transcendent, might make us want to adhere lightly to our beliefs and hold them tentatively. Yet that goes against the dynamics of any faith or ideology that wishes to claim truth.

---

[50] 1 Corinthians, 13, 12   [51] Akhtar, p. 61   [52] McKim, p. 29

A major answer to our perplexity when facing the transcendent could lie in the fact of human freedom. Those who complain about the hiddenness of God and His otherness, want justified certainty. Certainty must be bought at a price, and that price will be human freedom. If we cannot help believing in God and being sure of His nature, that means that any worship and reverence is a result of coercion. Perhaps some would prefer a world in which our destiny and course of life is not a matter of responsible choice. Some believe that we do live in a world where both belief and unbelief are equally predetermined. That, though, is a world in which we have no responsibility for the kind of people we are, or the choices we make. Without freedom of will, we become sophisticated automata. That may not be surprising in a godless world operating through chance. Given a monotheism, which sees humans of a special significance, it becomes more surprising. However imperfectly we may reflect the mind of the Creator, or His freedom in Creation, we should nevertheless expect that humans would have some control over their destiny, reflecting the freedom and the creativity of the Creator.

Epistemic distance, involving our inability to have complete knowledge of God, may make life and its decisions more precarious. It opens the possibility of varying understandings of the one God. We will fall into error. The more distant we are from the Godhead, the more likely we are come to different conclusions about its nature. We will come to different emphases about how God is to be approached, or worshipped. Given the positing of one God and one ultimate standard of truth, this must be a cause for concern. Some even wish to talk of the possibility of religious progress, and of gradual evolution in religious belief. Robert McKim, for example, argues for cooperation between different religions. He hopes that through mutual collaboration 'about how to make progress', we might be able to 'unearth possibilities that no one has yet considered'. Empirical science provides such a model, so that the fact of competing theories impels us to join in trying to obtain greater knowledge. McKim believes that this is the only possibility for religion 'if the human religious situation is ambiguous'.[53]

That vision goes against the self-understanding of the monotheistic religions with their claims to universality. McKim's idea of religious progress should not be restricted to monotheistic religions. Buddhism, for example, would want to join the conversation. The idea of one transcendent God is then made problematic, even more so once we take into account all the other religions held in the world. The idea of religious progress becomes a vote of 'no confidence' in any monotheistic claims.

---

[53] McKim, p. 51.

Humility about their limitations should be a characteristic of religious believers. Why, though, should anyone start to think in religious terms? We must still ask why they want to make claims about anything beyond the ordinary world of experience. Some have thought that religious beliefs are pre-scientific hangovers from an age when humans knew no better. Perhaps humans have now 'come of age', and can put such infantile concerns behind them. Individuals should put aside the simple beliefs with which they started off as children. That is the thought underlying the title of Richard Dawkins' book *Outgrowing God*.[54] He accepts that a tendency to think in religious terms lies deep in human nature. Though he characterises such beliefs as 'superstitious', he does not question their persistence. They perhaps involve what he dismissively called 'by-products' of other dispositions favoured by natural selection. Disagreement between religions just underlines, it will be said, that we should not rely on any of them. Yet this does not really address the question why humans looked for theistic explanations in the first place.

Religious disagreement is, above all, a disagreement about what is true. The assumption by atheists is still that there is a single standard of truth and falsity. The idea of one reality is itself a constituent element of monotheism. Without it, there is the danger that we are left with myriad beliefs, and no possibility, in principle, of ever seeing what is right. The problem is whether the idea of truth, that itself compels people to become dissatisfied with different forms of monotheism, has to be dissolved, once a belief is removed in the one God who is the source of everything, and the sole standard of truth.

4 The Roots of Religion

4.1 The Shadow of Monotheism

Without some conception that there could be a divine being or beings, communication from a divine reality would never be understood as such. We have also seen that the idea of a single standard of truth has been bound up with the conception of one God as its source. Obsession with diversity of human belief as the ultimate fact itself is incoherent, since there could then not be any ultimate facts. Even so, the undoubted fact of religious diversity still raises questions. Putting aside the problem of why a Creator allows diversity, why, given diversity, should monotheism be a preferred option? The political philosopher, John Gray, suggests that 'religion is universal, whereas monotheism is a local cult'.[55] This may use an anthropological perspective, but the remark does draw attention to the fact that while monotheism encourages us to think of one world,

---

[54] Dawkins, *Outgrowing God*   [55] J. Gray, *Seven Types of Atheism*, p. 4

that stance has not always been humanity's starting point. A belief in the ultimate unity of things has been the result of a development in human thinking, not its first assumption.

As Gray points out, basic presuppositions of Western civilisation are rooted in monotheism and its implications. Should we then question the foundations of the modern Western world? Even the turn to atheism has gained oxygen in a society saturated with theistic assumptions. Gray, himself an atheist, points out that the idea of the progress of humanity 'has replaced belief in divine providence', even though it depends on it.[56] Similarly the idea of a law-governed cosmos is derived from the idea of one ultimate lawgiver, but that basic assumption of science floats free of its original justification. The modern world is imbued with the idea of scientific progress, assuming a gradual growth of human knowledge because of the existence of a regular and ordered world. That idea gained its force because it was thought the world was created by God. The idea of a universal human rationality was much stressed by the seventeenth- and eighteenth-century Enlightenments. The irony is that it led to a 'rationalist' objection to religion through the power of a reason originally believed to have been the gift of God. Yet it originally depended on the idea of the divinely implanted power of reason (or *logos)* in human beings. That idea, stemming from Greek philosophy and adopted by Christianity, was intrinsically monotheistic.

The notion of the growth of knowledge derives from an idea of the linear development of human beings towards a destination. It contradicts the concept of a cyclical universe, as championed by some non-theistic religions. The possibility of a growth in knowledge suggests a truth that is not perpetually changing. It needs the fixed point as an ultimate standard that the God of monotheism has traditionally given. Popular sayings such as 'God only knows', and the philosophers' reference to a 'God's eye view' of things suggest that God is the fount of all knowledge. Indeed the atheist Nietzsche embraced a form of nihilism by upholding the eternal recurrence of everything.[57] Everything returns eternally without any improvement, progress, no notion of redemption or salvation, and no reason for guilt or regret. As Zarathustra says: 'I shall return internally to this identical and selfsame life, the greatest things and smallest, to teach once more the eternal recurrence of all things'.[58] Any idea of truth evaporates, to be replaced by the will to power. The way is made for the collapse of rational discussion, and of learning from each other. If there is nothing ultimately to learn, power and the exercise of will are all that are left.

---

[56] Gray, p. 1   [57] See Trigg, *Ideas of Human Nature*, ch. 10
[58] *Thus Spake Zarathustra*, p. 237

The issue is not then the content of our beliefs, or the reason or evidence we have. It becomes a question of what identity we claim. The roots of German fascism can be seen in some of Nietzsche's thought.

Gray points out that the idea of universal truth applying universally underpins the possibility of history. He suggests that it was only with Christianity that 'a history of humankind began to be told'.[59] He claims that before that, there was no universal history only stories of the Jews, Greeks and Romans and many others. Certainly the idea of a history unfolding towards some eschatological destination is intrinsically Christian. Yet some might feel that Gray is over-stating his case. There is a difference between myth and story on the one hand, and the careful chronicling of events as exemplified by Greek historians such as Thucydides on the other. Nevertheless, the basic point is that human nature, seen as a corollary of the divine nature, gives a universal vision that lifts us above the stories of particular people. The monotheism of the Jews often concentrated on their role as a chosen people. Yet claims to universality echo through Hebrew writings. Psalm 24, for instance, claims that 'to the Lord belong the earth and everything in it, the world and all its inhabitants'.

Gray's thesis is that 'secular thought is mostly composed of repressed religion'.[60] This is exemplified in the slogan of the French Revolution, *liberté, egalite, fraternite*. The eighteenth-century French Enlightenment quickly veered from theism, to deism and then outright atheism with a slavish devotion to 'Reason', no doubt in an attempt to remove the power of the Roman Catholic Church in France. Churches and cathedrals in France were for a time converted into 'Temples of Reason'. Yet a belief in human freedom makes little sense without a belief in free will, itself a legacy of Christian theology. Equality as a human ideal can only be underpinned with some idea of transcendent worth. Everyone may equally matter because we are all equal in the sight of God. Similarly, we have already mentioned that the idea of fraternity makes no sense without the idea of a common Father.

Western atheism still lies in the shadow of Christianity, retaining many of its assumptions without their justification. John Gray claims that ''contemporary atheism is a continuation of monotheism by other means'.[61] This is indicated in the much-respected idea of human rights. The drafters of the original United Nations Declaration of Human Rights in 1948 found it easier to agree on the rights to be recognised, than on why they were rights. Human rights are linked with the long-standing idea of natural rights, derived from an idea of our common humanity. The Declaration talks of the 'inherent dignity' and 'the equal and inalienable rights of all members of the human family'. Article 1

---

[59] Gray p. 28   [60] Gray, p. 72   [61] Gray, p. 158

refers to the fact that human beings are 'endowed with reason and conscience'. This suggests an objective order of morality built into the scheme of things. It is also hardly fanciful to see the further influence of monotheistic ways of thought. There seems to be one world, one humanity and one basic moral order. As humans, we are endowed with reason and conscience. The agent of this is unspecified, but the implication is that there is purpose at work, presumably by a Creator. The foundation of human rights is important, since an agreement about them, perhaps of a political nature, is never enough. That can be temporary. Rights have to be justified. Many in the world challenge the whole idea of human rights, perhaps as a Western construction. Rights gain their potency, because they are seen not as instruments of politics, but as derived from the scheme of things and the nature of our common humanity. The notion of rights challenges too easy an acceptance of basic diversity.

A basic moral order in the world, existing independently of the practices and beliefs of different cultures, is integral to the idea of monotheism. It is linked with the idea of purpose, or providence, inherent in the world. Yet an objective moral order depends on the assumption that the Creator of the universe is intrinsically good. Divine unity suggests that God's attributes are not a ragbag of unrelated properties. As Tim Mawson says in elucidating the idea of such unity, 'even if not all of God's uniquely identifying essential attributes notionally entail each other, they are all entailed by what it is to be the most perfect being possible'.[62] An evil Supreme Being could hardly fit in with any idea of perfection. However, the alleged moral order of the world often seems morally ambiguous. The venerable Problem of Evil rears its head. Any monotheism that assumes, as Christianity does, that its God is the source of moral perfection contends with this objection.

If there is no inherent purpose in the world, it will not be surprising that events occur which humans regard as terrible, because they threaten human interests. Dubbing them 'evil' sounds as if such they go against the grain of what is meant to be. In a world devoid of moral order, blind and pitiless, the introduction of a moral category such as 'evil' makes no sense. We may ask why God could allow such things. We have no grounds on which to object to them if there is no God and no purpose. The conviction that they cannot fit into any scheme of what should be stems from an impulse to monotheism. We may well wonder how far we should assume that a perfect God must act in ways that we think He ought to, but we cannot object to so-called 'evil' if there is no God. Everything would then ultimately be arbitrary and pointless, whatever meaning we try to give our own lives.

---

[62] T. Mawson, *The Divine Attributes*, p. 51

Deists might talk of order in the universe but still hold that God is unconcerned with the fate of human beings. Given the vastness of the universe, and even the possibility of extraterrestrial life, why should we matter? Must even a God, who embodies perfection, conform to our wills and wishes and be concerned about us? There seems to be a gap between the idea of God as an infinite creator with a purpose for His creation, and that of a God who cares for the inhabitants of this puny earth. It looks as if we need further knowledge about the nature of God.

What should motivate us to make sense of the conflicting claims of many religions? Monotheism may proclaim one universal truth, but why should we take any steps to making religious assumptions? The themes of the Enlightenment may have been derived from monotheism, but, in the eighteenth century, they soon bit the hand that had fed them. Reason and religion were seen as fundamentally opposed. Religion was dismissed as the product of authoritarian tradition, and reason seen as the vehicle of freedom, progress and improvement. Even in the twentieth century, in the 1960s, sociological theories saw secularism as an irresistible tide sweeping religion away. Such secularism, it was thought, was based on the inevitable increase in scientific knowledge. In the nineteenth century, in his memorable poem 'Dover Beach', Matthew Arnold talks of the sea of faith, which 'was once, too, of the full'. 'But', he continues, 'now I only hear its melancholy, long, withdrawing roar'. The image seemed apposite in the mid-twentieth century, at least in a Western Europe, exhausted by the Second World War.

It appeared that humans by nature did not need religion, because increased knowledge rendered such beliefs superfluous. This left unanswered the question what that knowledge rested on. Those who deny the universal scope of 'knowledge' and 'reason', seeing them as merely local products, may be on safer ground. Having given up monotheism, they are, like Nietzsche, not afraid to accept the consequences. Why, though, does every society appear to need religion? As archaeologists and anthropologists attest, religious beliefs have been a central feature of human groups.

4.2 The Cognitive Science of Religion

The relatively new discipline, 'the cognitive science of religion', has attempted to give scientific content to connecting religion and human nature.[63] Advocates of diversity stress the differences between human beings, and celebrate diversity as an end in itself. No doubt they are afraid of assuming their own views are

---

[63] For more on this and its implications see R. Trigg and J. Barrett (ed.), *The Roots of Religion: Exploring the Cognitive Science of Religion*

better than those of others, let alone suggesting that they know best. Yet this has to be self-defeating. The alleged fact of such social difference makes any universal science concerning human beings impossible. Doctrines of diversity claim themselves to be generalisations about human beings even though the idea of the human has already shattered into myriad pieces. The cognitive science of religion challenges this. It asserts that there is a common substructure beneath the cacophony of differences. Humans share natural predispositions across time and culture. Our common humanity is of greater significance than many students of society, whether sociologists or anthropologists, have some-times cared to admit. This view has been given impetus not just by neo-Darwinian theory, but by research into the human genome and the consequent tracing of basic human tendencies to particular forms of genetic make-up. The quest for, say, a single God-gene, bringing about a belief in God, is highly fanciful. The interaction between genes amongst themselves and their interac-tion, as a collection, with the environment is subtle. Empirical research shows that humans share natural dispositions that can form the building blocks of belief in the transcendent. The idea of a common human nature is crucial. It can act as a basic substratum for human societies, setting constraints and limits. All human societies have to face the same needs and necessities of human life. Different cultures may prefer different foods, but we all need food. The con-straints of human biology is constant across cultures. Poison in Washington, DC is poison in Beijing.

We understand those in other cultures, and understand their languages by accepting that we confront the same reality. As humans, we react in broadly similar ways to it, through common sensory systems. Otherwise, science becomes culturally specific with no universal relevance. Human reactions to the empirical world are broadly similar. That particularly applies to the way in which they are motivated to see the world with a religious perspective. This in no way argues that 'religion', or a particular religion, must be true since the diversity of religions cannot be ignored. Even so, tendencies to religious belief stem from what it is to be human and are not the quirk of a particular culture at a particular time. They are the product of the basic cognitive architecture of human beings.

This may explain the apparent universality of religion and indicates that religious belief is more 'natural', even than sophisticated, rational beliefs. Internal cognitive impulses may provide the building blocks of religious belief, and are our starting points as little children. Rational reflection, of the kind given by science or theology, is a second-order discipline reflecting on basic impulses which are often pre-rational and not consciously arrived at. To reason, we must have something to reason about, and instinctive, pre-rational beliefs give us the raw material. Further reasoning, perhaps through the rigours of scientific method, may make us realise that things are not so simple. An example in a non-religious context is our intuitive belief in the solidity of tables. Physical explanations in terms of subatomic particles suggest that solid objects are not solid at all. Those explanations may seem to go against common sense, and have to be taught. In the same way, theology can examine our starting points and intuitive responses to the world. It can place them in a wider context, perhaps even validating them in a more sophisticated way.

Another possible example is the immediate reaction of many to a neo-Darwinian contention that the world does not embody purpose, but is the result of chance genetic variations, which flourish, or not, according to the processes of natural selection. Those suited to their environment are the ones that survive and multiply. It is a causal process, the results of which we see and of which we ourselves are a product. There seems to be no direction, no purpose, no possibility of progress to anything better. Things just happen. Many people, not just theists, instinctively reject this, at least as a global theory. When a tragedy occurs, a natural human response is to ask why. People ask why such a thing should happen to them. Perhaps, more challengingly, we might ask why should it happen to anyone. The reply that all is chance seems unsatisfactory. Researchers into human cognition find that this is a deep-seated human response, stemming from automatic cognitive biases. Deborah Kelemen refers to what she terms the 'promiscuous teleology' of humans, who can unthinkingly ascribe purpose to anything.[64] We may want an explanation as to the origin of such biases, but that itself is derived from an assumption that things can be explained.

The quest for purpose and explanation is a normal human reaction. When asked why rocks, for instance, are pointed, children are unlikely to produce sophisticated theories of erosion. They will look for a purpose, and say something like 'it is so birds cannot sit on them'. Scientific studies have shown that, particularly under pressure of time, in speeded tests, even science graduates will unthinkingly react to a default position in terms of purpose. In biology, for instance, it is easy to say that the purpose of the heart is to pump blood round the body. That implies a specific design process, that would imply a designer. We are then on our way to a religious explanation, rather than a scientific one in causal terms.

4.3 A Universal Basis for Religion

An important objection to claims about what is natural to the human condition is the allegation of deep cultural bias. As has been stressed, we have all, whatever

---

[64] D. Kelemen, 'Function, Goals and Intention', *Current Trends in Cognitive Sciences*

our current beliefs, been brought up in a tradition and culture that is heavily influenced by monotheistic assumptions. Without realising, we may have taken on assumptions about purpose and progress that stem from theology. Is it surprising that, given this cultural background, our default beliefs are those we have imbibed, perhaps unconsciously, since childhood? Many are suspicious of reference to all things 'natural', and thereby fixed. In particular, they react vigorously against any suggestion that the roots of religion should be natural in human beings.

A scientific basis for examining this objection is to investigate attitudes in a society which has been uninfluenced by Western assumptions. Chinese culture has not been rooted in monotheism, and traditional assumptions there have not been formed by, say, the same cultural influences as in the United States. Experiments, however, have shown similar results to those in the West. Chinese participants defaulted to the notion that natural phenomena are purposefully designed when they were forced to make judgements at speed. The conclusion of one study says that 'the present results provide evidence of culturally recurrent, and potentially universal, cognitive tendencies to construe natural phenomena as purposefully made by an agent'. The study adds that 'this demonstrates that basic gut intuitions are independent of particular cultural constructs, and in particular the monotheistic belief in a Creator God'[65]. Universal tendencies to see things in a particular way are built into us all as humans. Monotheistic beliefs may fit such inclinations, but they are not necessarily responsible for them.

The cognitive science of religion must not jump to hasty conclusions. It can show why we find it easy to believe certain things but that does not prove that the beliefs are true (or false). Nevertheless, the moral must be that forms of relativism that maintain that all beliefs are culturally formed must be challenged. There appears to be a universal substructure of natural human reactions. Our minds are not blank slates on which any culture can write anything. Some beliefs will be more easily accepted than others. Modern cognitive science maintains that human minds are already inclined in certain directions.

Children may find even apparently complicated theological concepts easy to grasp, as is shown by a little experiment.[66] Take two cups, and put an apple under one, in front of a three-year-old child and the mother. When the mother goes out of the room, put the apple under the other cup, and then ask the child where Mummy will think it is when she comes back in. The child will say that the mother will know the new position, because he or she assumes that Mummy

---

[65] E. Järnefelt et al., 'Reasoning about Nature's Agency and Design in the Cultural Context of China', *Religion, Brain and Behavior*, 9, 2019

[66] I have done this with my twin grandchildren, separately.

knows everything. Try though the same experiment a year later, when the child's mind has developed further. Now the child will have what psychologists call a 'theory of mind', recognising that different people have different perspectives. No longer will it be assumed that Mummy knows everything, but the child will say that she will think the apple is still under the original cup because she had not seen it moved. Yet if you ask the child what God would know, the answer will quite likely come that God can know everything that happened and will know where the apple is. When asked why, children would say 'God knows everything' or 'God is God'.

A chorus of opposition will say that this shows how the children are being brought up, but that is not the point in question. What matters here is not what is true, or how children acquire beliefs. The question is what it is easy for even young human minds to grasp. Omniscience seems a tricky philosophical notion, but as this simple experiment indicates, there can be a progression from absolute faith in the all-knowing capabilities of one's mother, to the idea of an all-knowing God. The idea of someone knowing everything seems easy to grasp. Such building blocks of religious belief may be infantile. In the cool light of reason, we may question them. What cognitive science indicates is that they are basic to human life. We start with them, and they cannot be ignored. Religion, in its various guises, is deep-rooted.

Many studies in the cognitive science of religion demonstrate strands of human cognitive architecture that lead to religious belief. There is an inbuilt tendency in us to detect agency in events. If we hear a bump upstairs, we wonder who is there. When a tree rustles in the forest, we assume that an animal might be ready to spring at us. If we cannot see natural agents, we can posit supernatural ones, such as spirits. The power of the sea invited a belief in Poseidon. This facet of cognitive machinery has even acquired a name, HADD, a hypersensitive agency detection device.

Another natural reaction that can lead to belief in the supernatural is the fact that humans seem to assume a dualism of mind and body. Paul Bloom has described both children and adults as 'intuitive dualists'[67]. They seem able naturally to think of people ad surviving the death of their bodies. 'Religion', whatever that includes, does not come ready formed, but is the product of human dispositions to see things in particular ways. A willingness to look to a reality beyond this life, to unobservable agents, and to a purpose underlying everything are attitudes that can be classed as religious. Yet many different kinds of constructions can appear, given such building blocks. The cognitive science of religion may show significant tendencies in the way that humans naturally think, but they under-determine the beliefs that result. Humans may be naturally religious, in that they look beyond the physical world for explanations.

---

[67] P.Bloom, *Descartes' Baby*

This, though, does not provide one path to a particular kind of belief. Different outcomes are consistent with the same basic substructure.

4.4 Gods or God?

A predisposition to see supernatural agency does not necessarily entail that there is only one agent. Some have argued that polytheism is itself the natural default position for human beings. The positing of different forms of agencies such as tree spirits could lead in that direction. Against that, a strongly ingrained sense of purpose in the world, which is widespread, could lead to the idea that there would not be competing purposes but only an overarching one. That could lead to the notion of one Creator. The idea of omniscience itself leads to the idea of one omniscient Being who sees everything. As we have seen, the idea of competing omniscient beings, each of which knows everything about the others, is incoherent. Such beings would be indistinguishable.

We can be led in different directions by impulses we may hold in common. Truth cannot be settled by an appeal to universal attitudes; They can lead to easily to contradictory positions, such as polytheism and monotheism. A sense of the divine does not lead immediately to the idea of one God. Similar problems arise in discussions in contemporary philosophy of religion. Alvin Plantinga has followed the Reformer, John Calvin, in suggesting that there is a faculty, or cognitive mechanism, which in particular circumstances can trigger theistic beliefs. Plantinga's argument[68] is that they are basic beliefs that we start with, in the same way that we may have basic memory beliefs about what we had for breakfast, or about what we am now seeing. We may be mistaken but initially we take such beliefs on trust. We have what Calvin claimed is a *sensus divinitatis,* an awareness of divinity. That could tie in with claims by cognitive science that we do naturally envisage the supernatural beyond the natural, at least initially. The very abstraction of the idea of divinity, however, suggests a lack of religious specificity of the kind we encountered on the cognitive science of religion. It is dangerous to slide from the *sensus divinitatis* to a *sensus Dei,* an apprehension of one God. We then go too quickly from glimmerings of the transcendent to the God of monotheism, or even the God of Christianity.

We can see this move, tempting though it may seem, in the discussion by a philosopher of religion, Kelly Clark, of some of the implications of the cognitive science of religion. He notes, quite properly, that the term 'God-faculty' is in the context of cognitive science too specific. He accepts that such science is concerned with a conglomeration of faculties, including an

---

[68] See A. Plantinga, *Knowledge and Christian Belief,* p. 33

agency-detecting device and the theory of mind. He continues 'while these faculties could engender or mediate belief in God, as Plantinga conceives, they could also engender beliefs in elves, dwarves, goblins, tree spirits, and witches'. We may be all naturally disposed to believe in nonmaterial beings, but as Clark admits, 'these cognitive dispositions find culturally specific expression'.[69] We may be disposed naturally to be religious, but this does not provide an answer to the question which religion we should accept.

Having made the necessary qualifications, however, Clark immediately appears to forget them and launches into a discussion of the role of what he explicitly terms our 'God-faculty'. He suggests that if we 'are permitted to trust our cognitive faculties, and the God-faculty is one of those faculties, then we are permitted to trust the God-faculty and accept the beliefs produced by it'.[70] A universal human tendency to see things in a way that can lead to formalised religion may be plausible. Jumping from human nature to, say, the doctrines of Christianity requires argument. The cognitive science of religion does little to guide us to one religion amongst many. Talking of a God-faculty makes an illegitimate jump from a vague belief in spiritual beings, to a full-fledged monotheism.

As humans, we have an inclination towards the transcendent but no fully formed, or innate, beliefs about one God, or His nature. We have a readiness to hold religious beliefs, but little idea of what such beliefs might amount to. Major religions recognise this. They are all based on the assumption that further revelation is essential. Monotheism may depend on human readiness to look to the divine. It also needs God, as transcendent, to reveal Himself in terms that humans can understand. There would be no need for special revelation if we all initially had fully formed and specific religious beliefs in some form of general revelation. There would then be no epistemic distance allowing us to be free to make our own choices. There could, indeed, then be no genuine human freedom.

A world without human freedom, where everyone is programmed to have true beliefs, and act accordingly, might seem attractive. It would not be our world, and its agents would be mere automata without personal responsibility, or even a proper awareness of the difference between good and evil. Freedom is a basic human trait, and too much stress on cultural difference, and the formative role of culture, can obscure this. We are free to question the assumptions of our own culture and religious outlook, as much as to criticise those of others. We should do so, as it is only through such questioning that we can test, and perhaps confirm, the truth that otherwise we would take for granted.

---

[69] K. J. Clark, *God and the Brain*, p. 75   [70] Clark, p. 77

An indispensable partner of human freedom is the ability of humans to reason. That does not mean that all humans should be would-be philosophers. It means that everyone can question what they are told, and decide for themselves what they should accept. Such freedom, however, must not be confused with the ideal of autonomy that often accompanies an extreme individualism. Freedom allows us to recognise what is true, or reject it. It not only coexists with, but gains its purpose from, the idea of an objective truth. Autonomy, however, demands that it decides for itself what should be true. My standards may not be yours, and each is valid for the holder. Criticising another would infringe on that person's autonomy.

Some imagine that the idea of objective truth constrains us in a way that nullifies human freedom. Is the freedom to be in error that valuable? Does error have any rights? These questions become more pressing when confronted with the power of an all-seeing God. Is not the idea of one God, and one objective truth, itself oppressive? This is the question to which we must now turn.

5 Monotheism and Truth

5.1 Truth and Coercion

Relativism may seem to encourage the toleration of difference. If a group is right in their own eyes, why should anyone else presume to impose alien standards on them? If there is no such thing as being right, I cannot criticise those with different views. Yet it is difficult to state this consistently. I cannot simultaneously deny the idea of truth, and recognise the truth that many people hold different beliefs and have different practices from me and my society. Further, religions typically claim that truths hold not just for believers, but also for those who reject them. If religious beliefs cannot claim to be universally true, nobody has reasons to go on believing. I should not accept beliefs merely because I, or because others, take them for granted. Unless they have some claim on everyone, why should I myself recognise them as valid? Relativism is corrosive for all religious belief, rendering it a mere empty shell.

The idea, too, that relativism encourages toleration must be questioned. A society may impose its assumptions and way of life on others, because its nature is to be authoritarian and imperialistic. Difference may be a source of antagonism, even if there is no rational grounding for it. Toleration is an ethical principle, derived from a world outlook that accepts the intrinsic dignity and freedom of others, even when their beliefs might seem repugnant. Yet respect for dignity and freedom, and the ensuing respect for difference and diversity, is far from widespread. It itself needs rational grounding.

Critics will still be worried by the implications of a belief in an objective truth which ought to be accepted by all because universally valid. Should not those in error be then corrected for their own good? Belief in the God of monotheism seems vulnerable to this criticism simply because it maintains the ideas of one truth and one reality, against which people's beliefs must be measured. Some would say that the idea of one truth is totalitarian. If I claim to know what people ought to believe, may not I have a positive duty to ensure that everyone holds the right views? An old tag asserts that 'error has no rights', and that attitude has influenced some religious positions. The Roman Catholic Inquisition cared little for the rights of an individual conscience. Truth, as seen by the Church, had to be secured and imposed. This treatment was usually restricted to baptised members of the Church, particularly for alleged heresy. It is an approach that has been championed in secular contexts. Lenin, for instance, believed passionately in realism, upholding the existence of one objective world.[71] He wanted to ensure deviant political beliefs about its nature would be outlawed. The imposition of orthodoxy is thus not the preserve of different religions. The desire to make other people think like us, whoever we are, is widespread. Even in a society imbued with relativist views, majority public opinion can be eager to quash minority views that are out of step with the rest of society.

It is too easily assumed that, given an objective world, humans can have definite knowledge of it, and an ensuing right, even a duty, to impose that knowledge on others. Toleration seems to some to imply that we do not really know what is true ourselves. Allowing the practice of apparently deviant beliefs seems to imply lack of confidence in the truth of one's own. This outlook can have both political and religious consequences. In contemporary Russia, for example, the Russian Orthodox Church is unwilling to accept apparent competitors, particularly if they seem to have foreign money behind them. Orthodox Protestant churches, such as the Methodist Church, have come under attack in Russia, because their origins lie outside Russia. Only the Orthodox Church, it seems, can embody the spirit of Russia properly. The test seems to be the integrity of the nation, not the nature of truth. This view, however, seems to be sinking into the very relativism the Orthodox Church despises.

We have to recognise the objectivity, the 'otherness' of truth, and accept the epistemic distance, already referred to, that seems to exist between God and ourselves. This gap means that others in good conscience may not agree with us. Truth does not entail our omniscience. Just because there is something to agree about does not entail we achieve agreement. Monotheistic religions assert a truth that all should recognise universally, but, given human fallibility, that

---

[71] See Trigg, *Reality at Risk*, 2nd ed., ch. 2.

is not an aim that will be achieved. Christianity recognises this, and stresses the sin that makes us go astray following our own interests. It encourages us to be humble in our estimation of our abilities, and its focus on human free will encourages us to respect the free choices of others.

There is a significant step from preaching and rational persuasion to coercion. An imperative for mission follows from the idea of the universality of truth. Yet an impetus to share one's beliefs about what is true must respect the freedom of others. If the idea of truth both depends on, and demands, that of human freedom, preaching has to respect that freedom. Belief in it acknowledges that preaching can be rejected as well as accepted. We must not forget the logical distance between the idea of objective truth, and the intolerant imposition of one set of standards. Just because there is an objective state of affairs does not mean that we know it. It may be about to rain, but I may still go out without a raincoat. The simple gap between truth and knowledge, or even belief, applies all the more when we face, as finite beings, the immensity of any transcendent reality. By definition, it will be almost beyond our understanding. We may perhaps be rationally confident in our knowledge, but there is a further stage in our approach to other people. We will have reached apparent certainty because of our own freedom to accept or reject possibilities. We ought, therefore, to respect other people's freedom to disagree with us by doing the same.

So far from the espousal of objective truth leading to some form of totalitarianism, it is likely to lead to the recognition, and even the nurturing, of the existence of different viewpoints in a pluralist society. This has, at times, been a hard lesson to learn for monotheistic religions, as they preach of the one God who is the source of all truth. Some elements of Islam similarly exhibit intolerance of alternative positions, both within and outside Islam. The Christian Church, as mentioned already, has been tempted at times to use a position of power to restrain perceived heresy, regardless of individual conscience. Cynics have often remarked that when the Church, or even individual Christians, feel weak, they talk about freedom, and when they feel strong, they talk about truth. If people can play an influential role in their own country, they are less concerned about the importance of individual freedom than if they are 'nonconformists' or 'dissenters' as part of an unpopular minority. Yet the exercise of power and the pursuit of it should be very different.

5.2 Truth and Freedom

A particular example arises from the writings of Thomas Helwys in the reign of James I of England at the beginning of the seventeenth century. An early Baptist, he put forward the first modern argument upholding the idea of religious liberty. He claimed that all should choose their religion for themselves, and gave a theological argument: 'They only must stand themselves before the judgement seat of God to answer for themselves, when it should be no excuse to say that we were commanded or compelled to be of this religion by the King or by them that had authority over him'.[72] King James was not convinced by Helwys and his sometimes intemperate language, and Helwys ended his days in prison. At that time, religion was irretrievably mixed up with the threat of rebellion, as was witnessed by the Gunpowder Plot to blow up Parliament in 1605. That was itself widely seen as the product of Catholic agitation against the Protestant King James.

As a Baptist, Helwys was part of a small minority that did not wish to conform with the religious practices of the day. The advocacy of freedom was in their interests, as it was not in that of King James or the government. Nevertheless, Helwys was arguing for freedom in the things of religion in a way that was not pragmatic or political. It was unashamedly theological. God demands, he held, that we take responsibility for ourselves and answer to Him for our beliefs and practices. This view was taken up later in the same century by John Locke in his pleas for toleration. Conformity and orthodoxy are unimportant compared with personal commitment and the integrity of the individual. The freedom of conscience thus demanded, with our concomitant responsibility to God for right decisions, is rooted in respect of a truth. The arbiter, however, of such truth is the individual, and not the King, Church authorities such as bishops, or whoever else is in a position of power to impose their will. Freedom is explicitly opposed to power.

This is a theme that has been much present in some modern philosophy. Some philosophers have decried the very notion of metaphysics as 'totalising'. Metaphysics, it seems, sets standards all ought to accept, rather than embracing diversity in religion or beyond. Yet the paradox is that a religion without metaphysics, without the ability to sketch a picture of an underlying reality, becomes a religion that is nothing more than the outcome of subjective taste. The Italian philosopher Gianni Vattimo talks of 'a dislocation of the idea of truth, towards the idea of charity, respect, and of listening to the other'.[73] This is in the spirit of the post-modernist view that truth is historically situated, and is the production of consensus at particular times and places. Truth is not then regarded as a reflection of how things are, let alone grounded in a God above place and time. Vattimo imagines that a quest for agreement, rather than some

---

[72] T. Helwys, *A Short Declaration of the Mystery of Iniquity*, p. 37
[73] G. Vattimo, *Of Reality*, p. 170

universally valid notion of absolute truth, would somehow free us from a preoccupation with power.

Yet even if we grant that monotheism can sometimes produce a dangerous certainty and intolerance of apparent error, the loss of an aspiration to universalism does not help. We are left with conflicting sets of agreements, perhaps even conflicting religions, or differences of religious interpretation within one religion. How can such situations be resolved? Without any possibility of an appeal to a rationality we can all share, or a common reality to which we can all in principle have access, there is no way towards reconciliation. There is by definition nothing to agree about, beyond the fact of agreement, if we can still talk about facts. What would such an agreement, or consensus, in such a situation amount to? What could it be based on? An obvious response would be the exercise of power, and even force, to make sure others conform to our wishes.

The removal of the unitary idea of truth is unlikely to further the cause of the reconciliation of differences. Indeed, if reason could be seen as the shadow of the one God, attacks on the idea of God are very likely to end in the realisation that the idea of universal standards of reason is just as problematic. The slide from the universalism of the Enlightenment to the relativism of post-modernism was perhaps inevitable. Once monotheism was challenged, the path to nihilism was smooth. Even Vattimo admits that the idea that every assertion ought to aim for universal validity 'is probably an inheritance not only of rationalism (from the Greeks or the eighteenth century) but also of Christianity'.[74] The idea of objective truth both leads to, and stems from, monotheism. Without the notion of one God, human knowledge will easily fragment. Indeed, as Nietzsche himself recognised, it is bound to do so. We are left with a cacophony of diverse beliefs, in which we are all caught up.

Yet many will still question the possibility of resolving conflict through the principles of monotheism, rather than condemning monotheism for the conflict. It brings us back to the perennial issue why the one God should be so hidden. Why should it be so difficult to get agreement? While polytheism can accept diversity, through its standard of universal truth, monotheism is rooted in the idea of a basic unity. Diversity, and religious belief above all, must always be a basic challenge. Judaism, with its concentration on the idea of a chosen people, may not find this is as much of a problem as do Christianity and Islam, with their own unashamedly universalist claims and their eagerness to proselytise. Even so, Jewish writings, such as the Psalms, look to the day when 'all the nations' shall recognise the one God.

---

[74] Vattimo, p. 163

Islam has traditionally been ready to spread its idea of the one truth through conquest, as have branches of Christianity at times. Yet all the monotheistic religions have to produce explanations for religious diversity from their own theological resources. Why is there is one truth, and one God, but many beliefs? We have already referred to the fact that if humans are made in the 'image of God', they cannot be mere automata but have to take responsibility for themselves. They are also limited beings, with partial knowledge. Christians, however, with the idea of original sin, have suggested that we were even born, as humans, with a bias towards our own interests at the expense of others. This tallies with neo-Darwinian theories of the way organisms, including humans, have to pursue their interests, particularly relating to survival and reproduction, if their genes are to spread. Some would also stress the need for cooperation within a group to enable flourishing. Whatever the arguments about the merits of such individual, or group, selection, self-denying altruism certainly goes against our immediate biological interests. Any wish to pursue the interests of others will be at great cost to ourselves, and perhaps inhibit the spread of genes encouraging such behaviour. It seems that basic tendencies in our biological nature may always encourage the pursuit of self-interest.

Various religions act as counterweights to this innate selfishness, but the fact that they all coexist bears witness to the limited understanding of humans. Whatever our tentative yearning for a divine explanation, the sense of the divine is left under-determined by our nature. The basic issue facing monotheism is that we are often confronted with what are apparently diverse, even contradictory revelations of the one God. It may be difficult to resolve how far they are each reliable, but given that there is one God, one Creator of the universe, one purpose of the nature of things, revelations that are genuinely contradictory cannot all be right. Perhaps they contain partial understandings and we must have the humility to understand that we cannot as humans see the whole picture. If we could, we would ourselves be omniscient, and would ourselves be God. The trick is to be tolerant, and respectful, of those trying to tread a path to true belief. It is a toleration that should not extend to weakly accepting that there are many truths, any more than that there are many gods.

Just because others disagree, we should not be diverted from to trying to obtain what we consider to be the most adequate understanding of what is true. Even in the physical sciences, there is plenty of disagreement at the frontiers of knowledge, where empirical research gives out. The scientific response is not to say that what humans cannot understand is not real, but to press on patiently to greater understanding. With new theories, and new technology, things may become clearer. This may not provide an exact analogy for religion. However, diversity and disagreement over religious matters should never be the occasion for giving up, or for lapsing into scepticism, or worse, nihilism. Truth is still at stake.

5.3 Disunity within Religions

Diversity of belief does not warrant a conclusion that there is nothing to have beliefs about. Our own inadequacy as humans is more likely to be at the heart of the problem. Yet still the idea of one God suggests that, in principle at least, there should be one set of beliefs. We have an ideal of unity and are confronted with diversity. This is not just a problem for alternative, even competing, theistic beliefs held by different religions. It is a problem within the different monotheistic religions. Judaism, Islam and Christianity, are all disfigured by splits and divisions. The fracture between Sunni and Shia Muslims is of particular relevance, because of its present-day political repercussions. Judaism presents a far-from-united face with divisions, for instance, between liberal and Orthodox Jews whose ways of life can be very different.

The divisions between different branches of Christianity may be less rancorous than they once were, but they still exist. The old Protestant denominations are now more like fossils, representing the disagreement of previous centuries, frozen in institutional form. Nowadays, as in Judaism, the fractures are more likely to occur between liberal and conservative understandings of the Christian faith. Should Christians, for instance, conform to modern, secular understandings of human life and sexuality, or keep to the traditional moral teaching of centuries? Should ancient metaphysical understandings about the nature of God to be made to conform to contemporary scientific understanding, which itself will inevitably change? Does the Bible contain timeless truths of great relevance to us today, or is it itself the product of a culture radically different from our own, and to be understood as such?

It is no part of this Section to resolve such tensions, but to point out that as disagreements increase and arguments in religious institutions mount, it is easy even within a particular religion to forget how monotheism implies unity and not diversity. As is the case with the other monotheistic religions, as they struggle with different factions, the more the unity of the Church itself is torn asunder, the less the Christian religion is going to reflect the nature of the one God. One Christian hymn repeats the refrain, as something of a, cry, 'one Church, one Faith one Lord'. That must be the undoubted theory behind a monotheistic religion. Its practitioners should reflect within their worship and their lives something of the unity of the Godhead. If there is one source of truth that sets the sole standard of what should be believed, unity of belief should be the undoubted aim. Disunity and disagreement both imply error, whether wilful or not. That does not mean there will be no cultural and other differences within the practice of different religions. Within a broad unity, there is room for difference, reflecting deep cultural differences. What is regarded as appropriate dress and diet, for example, can vary, just as worship can take place with different styles and in different languages. Yet, in the case of Christianity, for instance, something is going very wrong if Christians are at odds with each other over the basic truths they wish to teach.

A Hindu once said to a Christian: 'How can you preach a gospel of love and reconciliation when you cannot be reconciled with your fellow Christians?' That is an unanswerable question. Christians who are content with the divisions, must either be hypocrites, or they do not genuinely believe in the oneness of God. The beliefs and practices they hold become more important than the God they pretend to worship. Division and disagreement become more acceptable than any view of the one reality that exists for everyone.

Monotheism cannot coexist with good conscience with the fact of religious diversity. Division may be a fact of human life, and one that can produce different religions. Within what purports, however to be one religion, there ought to be even more discomfort about it. We have repeatedly seen how some emphasise the role of power in society. The Christian Church, like any other institution, is susceptible to manipulation by the powerful. Yet once the Church, however defined, becomes a mere instrument of power, the idea of objective truth has been jettisoned, together with the monotheism that insists on one standard of truth. Christians should aim to portray, as best they can, that truth to the world. The more that divisions are created, the more they begin to betray their own vision. A particular concern is the systematic confusion between what is essential to, say, Christian belief, and what is of peripheral importance. It is all too easy to see what is familiar as essential. Even the layout of a building for worship and its architecture can acquire the importance of a basic article of faith.

There is a constant temptation in any social grouping to enforce agreement and to be intolerant of diversity. The dangers of division and disintegration within any institution might seem to suggest the importance of uniformity. No society can exist in which everyone is left to do what is right in their own eyes or believe what they wish. Churches, together with nations, have to balance the demands of human freedom against the need for a discipline that can hold a particular society together. A society without any rules, or laws, is no society at all. Even golf clubs realise that. The paradox is that however important dissent might be for the possibility of human freedom, some uniform social structures are also necessary for the maintenance of our life together in whatever context. A balance has to be struck.

We have already mentioned how John Locke, the great advocate of toleration, particularly in religious matters, was opposed to coerced belief. Like Helwys, Locke believed that the way to salvation was not 'any forced exterior performance, but the voluntary and secret choice of the mind'.[75] Locke claims that whether divisions are between religions or within Christianity, we should not force our opinions on others. He says that to force others to our mind, will be out of 'pride or of a weakness of my own opinion, and a secret conceit of my own infallibility, taking to myself something of a godlike power'. That, for Locke, was the product of a 'depraved, ambitious, human nature'.[76]

Locke's views of toleration have had enormous influence, not least through the influence of his writings a hundred years later on Thomas Jefferson, and on the ideas behind the Founding of the United States. He was an advocate of 'latitudinarianism'. In England, that was a plea for a Church of England that was comprehensive enough to contain the dissenters, who in Locke's lifetime were being forced to leave that Church. It is a warning about the enforcement of too-tight a uniformity, not just in ways of worship, such as whether clergy should wear white surpluses or black gowns, but also in beliefs that could be regarded as peripheral.

5.4 The Limits of Toleration

This raises large issues, within both the Christian Church and wider society, about the limits of toleration. How much latitude should really be given to private, subjective apprehension of what is true? The latter can seem to be upheld by appeals to freedom of conscience. Just, however, as a society has to rest on some minimum agreement between its citizens, a religious institution such as a Church, must have some standard of belief to be a cohesive institution. As with any society, it must achieve agreement about which beliefs, however few, are of central importance. Locke, in his treatise significantly titled *The Reasonableness of Christianity*, seemed to think the belief that 'Jesus is the Messiah', coupled with repentance, was what was of central importance.[77] There is, however, still room for disagreement about the full implications of this.

For a society to be recognised as a community with things in common, there has to be some agreement about its basic principles and what should be taught to children. A community is more than a group of people who happen to be in the same place at the same time. Hundreds of people hurrying across an airport

---

[75] J. Locke P.138. 'An Essay on Toleration', in *Political Essays*, ed. M. Goldie, p. 138

[76] Locke, ' An Essay in Toleration', p. 139

[77] J. Locke, *The Reasonableness of Christianity*, p. 105

concourse, composed of many nationalities and different languages, many in transit, and merely changing planes, do not constitute a community. Tourists thronging a famous cathedral do not constitute a religious community, even if they are in a religious building together. If all people are left to form their own best estimate of truth, with no dialogue, teaching or learning, the result is bound to be that everyone will be in a church, or other institution, of one member, or even a nation of one person.

Imposition of belief does not respect individual freedom or, in religious contexts, the responsibility of each person to the one God. On the other hand, an extreme subjectivism encourages the breakdown of communities and societies, and the destruction of all religious institutions, such as Churches. Without an agreed-upon basis for how society should be organised, and a minimum standard of belief for membership, there can be no basis for cooperation or collective endeavour. Religions, any religions, encapsulate what people think most important in life. It is inevitable, therefore, that religious beliefs can never be an optional extra, but will always be involved with the foundations of the shared assumptions of any given society. The nature of even a secular society will never be entirely separate from religious contributions to it.

The enforcement of shared standards not only fails to respect individual freedom. It can never work as effectively as when people actually themselves believe in the shared assumptions on which the society is based. A dedicated Nazi, or Communist, who really believes in an ideology, is much more dangerous than a cowed population paying lip service to beliefs and practices they know are not well based. The latter was the situation in countries such as Hungary in the dying days of communism. Once the threat of Russian tanks was removed, the whole system immediately collapsed, like a pack of cards. No one believed in it.

Personal religious faith, shared by many, is undoubtedly a significant feature in providing the glue that holds a society together. Yet just because it has to be personal and sincere, it can encourage an extreme individualism that insists that 'my' truth is 'the truth', so I become unwilling to listen to, let alone compromise with, others I have to live with. Radical proponents of freedom, perhaps claiming to rely on some 'inner light', can champion their idea of truth by insisting that they alone have a monopoly of it. We have mentioned Thomas Helwys, and not only King James was a target in his book.[78] Helwys was vitriolic in his condemnation of all religious authorities. Perhaps it would be expected that he would attack the Roman Catholic Church, and even the Bishops of the Church of England for their authoritariansm. However, he did

---

[78] Helwys, *A Short Declaration of the Mystery of Iniquity*

not have a good word to say about his fellow dissenters in the ranks of the Puritans of his age. Presbyterians and Independents (later Congregationalists), came in for fierce criticism. No one else, it seemed could possibly measure up to his own standards. Roger Williams, the founder of the Colony of Rhode Island, was of a similar ilk a few years later.[79] An impressive proponent of freedom, and of the separation of church and state, he started off as an ordained clergyman in the Church of England, but emigrated to join the Puritans of Massachusetts. They expelled him because of his dangerous opinions, but he never really settled as a Baptist either. His upholding of religious freedom verged on an anarchic repudiation of all organised religion.

We seem to be trapped between the imposition of authoritarian standards to maintain cohesion, and a claim to truth by each individual regardless of other opinions. The first position is often named theocracy, but if societies really were to be governed by God perhaps that would, by definition, be no bad thing. The Christian idea of heaven may envisage precisely that kind of society. God, however, rarely rules in human societies, because human intermediaries often interpret the wishes of God in ways that may be erroneous, self-interested, or perhaps both. Yet the alternative seems at best unstable, if it could even exist in the first place. Roger Williams was one of the earliest proponents of the idea of the separation of church and state, which became so important in the development of the United States. Might that be an answer? If organised society were neutral toward religious principles, we would be free to worship as we please, as long as we conform to agreed standards of life together. We could preserve a personal freedom of conscience, it might appear, while avoiding Thomas Hobbes' 'war of all against all'.

The neutrality of the state towards religious matters is the fundamental proposition of a liberal society, which tries to obtain cohesion while recognising fundamental disagreement. Yet this has the effect of downgrading all religion, so that it becomes a matter of personal decision and commitment, not of universal import. It implies that religious views can say nothing of relevance about the way that society ought to be organised to enable its citizens to flourish. The view treats religious commitment as an expression of a subjective taste of an individual. Some people like to play golf at weekends, while others go to church, synagogue or mosque. There is no implication that any of this affects the wider welfare of society. Just because Roger Williams trod such an extreme subjectivist path, he could quite easily separate church and state. The implication would be that nothing the churches, or any religious organisation, might say

---

[79] See R. Trigg, *Religious Diversity*, p. 139ff.

could be of relevance to our common life together. Religious diversity is thus dealt with by marginalising all religion.

Serious practitioners of any monotheistic religion could not in all consistency accept this. The one God cannot both be worthy of worship, and totally disinterested in how we live and behave. One God, as we have seen, should imply one foundation for what is good and right. Monotheism cannot have any truck with a kind of pluralism that says either that there are no fixed standards or principles, or that there are different alternative ones. Toleration of different views, and respect for them is not the same as imagining that what you believe does not matter. Human nature is derived from the will of the one God, according to monotheism, who, it is said, made us in His own image. What is good or bad for us, what enables us to flourish or can destroy us, depends on the nature of the creation of the one God. How we decide to treat each other must be connected with our understanding of this. Our religious beliefs, or repudiation of them, will influence our views about what is good or bad for society, and what, in a democracy, we should advocate. A democracy that shuts off all arguments which rely on religious insights fails to take seriously what many of its members consider most important in life. Religion cannot be excluded from public life in the name of freedom, as this is to challenge the freedom of citizens to live by their most basic beliefs and to advocate them.

5.5 Religion and Society

Some will react with horror to this, as it seems to import into public debate the disagreements and rancour of private religion. Yet democracy is only necessary in the first place because of disunity and division. There will be problems if we pretend that they just do not exist. Religious views of whatever kind – good or bad, true or false – are better aired than left to fester in hidden places. They can then be faced, and perhaps challenged and argued with. The appeal to liberalism, and by implication to freedom, as a bulwark against religion, is dangerous. Just because religion is so deeply rooted in human nature, and can arouse such passions, it is vital that religious voices be heard, and freedom of religion not constrained. Those with a strong religious commitment should never be afraid of appeals to public reason, unless they are arbitrarily restricted to matters within the reach of science. That restriction begs the question against religion. Human rationality is part of what makes us human. Truth is not just universally valid, but in principle universally accessible, even if we, as humans, can only obtain partial glimpses of it. The seventeenth century slogan echoes down the centuries that reason is a gift of God, 'the candle of the Lord'. If we think we have a grasp on what is true, we should not be afraid of letting our beliefs be open to challenge in the public sphere. As John Stuart Mill says in *On Liberty* talking about the 'wise man': 'The steady habit of correcting and completing his own opinion by collating it with those of others, so far from causing doubt and hesitation in carrying it into practice, is the only stable foundation for just reliance on it'.[80] We have a good reason for being ready to listen to others, when we disagree. The alternative is to claim an easy omniscience for ourselves.

Many will object that this is to make religion, any religion, too much a matter of reason. Surely, they will say, faith is not the same thing as reason. Faith is personal and subjective. It is something about me and my 'values'. It is not primarily concerned with the world. That is precisely the view being opposed, since it says that religion has no purchase in public life. It holds that my particular religion says everything about me and my priorities and commitments, but nothing about the human condition. It denies that any religious view is attempting to manifest a truth that is universally valid and important. There are political reasons for marginalising religion. The State need not get involved in tiresome theological and metaphysical disputes that it is ill-equipped to deal with. In trying to be tolerant and not sit in judgement on personal faith, it can reduce all religion to the status of harmless hobby, and not the would-be purveyor of the most important truths that humans ought to face. It also means that those who think that some religion, or even all religion, is harmful are not allowed to say that in public debate.

Religious diversity creates undoubted problems for a pluralist society, particularly when, perhaps through immigration, there may be different religions clamouring for attention. The difficulties are not in principle greater than when a State is confronted with competing Christian denominations. In England, religious disagreement was a factor in the seventeenth-century Civil War between King and Parliament. Since 1689, however, it has been recognised that citizenship and religious affiliation do not go together in England. The Act of Toleration recognised that distinction. Since then, people with different views about religion have been gradually able to play a full part in public life and debate. Membership of the Established Church no longer remained a requirement for participation. This was achieved through recognising and respecting the differences between citizens, without prohibiting them from taking a public stance about the things they believed in. The influence they had thus largely depended on their ability to convince others

---

[80] J. S. Mill, 'On Liberty', in *Utilitarianism*, ed. M. Warnock, p. 146

about what ought to be done. Freedom, and the ensuing diversity, need not be the enemies of truth. Disagreements about what is the case, and what ought to be done, gain their saliency from the fact that much is at stake. The effects of whatever public policies are adopted can often be later shown to be disastrous or beneficial.

Institutional religion can come under criticism for solidifying intolerance and hostility to those outside. It is sometimes seen as the enemy of individual freedom. Institutions have set doctrines and rules, hierarchies and an apparent exercise of power. Individuals, however, on their own, cannot themselves preserve particular forms of teaching without associating with others. The more diversity there is in a society, the more vital this becomes. The transmission of beliefs through the generations needs some form of institutional base to ensure continuity and consistency. Orthodoxy, as seen by particular bodies of teaching, needs support. In religious institutions, as well as the wider society, referred to by Mill in *On Liberty,* everyone needs to 'collate' their beliefs with those of others. Otherwise we all are liable to sink into the morass o a subjectivism that can lead to anarchy and nihilism.

Freedom can be cherished through the right of any individual to join, or leave, particular religious institutions. People who are born into a particular religion, because their parents were adherents, should not thereby be trapped in it. The existence of religious institutions guarantees the survival of bodies of teaching, but they should have no rights of compulsion over their members, unless they choose to be members. At times, the Roman Catholic Church has tended to assume that if you were born, and baptised, a Catholic, you are always a Catholic. That attitude has waned, but it still remains strong in the context of some Islamic countries, where you are regarded as always a Muslim, if you were born one. Leaving Islam is counted as apostasy and can be punished by death.

Religious freedom implies the rights of the individual conscience, and the freedom to manifest one's personal beliefs. A stress on freedom appeals to deep tendencies in human nature. It is not just a Protestant idiosyncrasy. Yet, as we see, there is also need for an association of like-minded people in settled institutions. This is true of all activities. I cannot play golf or enjoy cricket on my own but need a club to join. The club, in turn, will have its rules for what constitutes playing the game properly. Individual freedom consists in deciding which clubs to join, and not the demand that I myself will decide what counts as cricket. Also crucial is the ability of people to join or leave particular religions or religious institutions. It is not for an individual alone to decide what counts as a proper interpretation of Islam. An individual should be free, however, to decide whether to be a Muslim or not, even if they were born of Muslim parents.

The need for religious institutions to be able to set their own standards and enforce them on those who choose to be members should not be remarkable. No genuinely free society should fail to protect such institutions, even when they diverge from the fashionable assumptions of the day. The same dynamic applies in the empirical sciences. We need a balance both between individual insight and the collective judgement of others. An individual scientist may apparently make a remarkable discovery, but it will need corroboration through repeated experiments and observations, and acceptance rather scientists. Then it can gain traction, and perhaps eventually become part of the teaching of orthodox science.

An imperative for any nation or state is to achieve social cohesion, and the temptation is to achieve this through uniformity of belief and practice. Too much diversity can threaten the foundations of any community. The temptation is either to enforce conformity, the way of totalitarian government, or to give up and let a society dissolve into different groups, all struggling for power. Neither is acceptable and the only path is for mature democracies to allow the maximum amount of freedom to different beliefs and practices, while recognising that truth is still at stake and that dialogue between different standpoints is essential. The same dynamic must apply within the broad ambit of religion. People must, as far as possible, be free to live their lives according to different beliefs. Yet acquiescence in the fact of diversity, and perhaps even the celebration of religious diversity as an end in itself, can never be right. If we passively accept that each group, or even each person, holds to what is true for them, we are betraying the idea of the one truth. Yet the latter concept is the property and legacy of monotheism. Society still needs the vision that there cannot be many alternative realities. There is only one reality. If 'God' is simply a human construction or projection, the atheist is right. There can be no God. The paradox is that even that assertion points to the theistic notion that there is one truth, even though it entails the denial of God's existence. There is then the tacit assumption that there is one reality, but not a reality that includes God. It has been the contention of this Element that this is a fundamentally unstable position. It involves an atheism still influenced by the presuppositions of monotheism.

The challenge ultimately is not so much why the one God allows diverse beliefs. Given the Judaeo-Christian belief that humans are free and responsible for their choices, there can be an explanation for that. The crucial issue is how there can be any unity behind diversity without some universal, unifying principle. The one God of monotheism, the Creator of all that there is, has historically fulfilled that role. A monotheistic belief can continue to do so. The alternative has to be irresolvable clashes between rival worldviews, or even subjective opinions. The only recourse can then be the unprincipled use of power. Rationality would then be an illusion. Might would be the only source of right. Personal abuse will be the inevitable substitute for reasoned discussion.

Bibliography

Akhtar, S. (2018). *The New Testament in Muslim Eyes: Paul's Letter to the Galatians*, London: Routledge

Barth, K. (1957). *Church Dogmatics: Vol 2 The Doctrine of God*, Edinburgh: T & T Clark

Bloom P., (2004) Descartes' Baby: How the Science of Child Development Explains What Makes Us Human, New York, Basic Books

Clark, K.J (2019). *God and the Brain: The Rationality of Belief*, Grand Rapids, MI: Eerdmans

Dawkins, R. (2019). *Outgrowing God*, London: Bantam Press

Gray, J. (2018). *Seven Types of Atheism*, London: Allen Lane

Helwys, T., ed. (1998). *A Short Declaration of the Mystery of Iniquity*, Macon, GA: Mercer University Press

Hick, J. (1989). *An Interpretation of Religion*, Basingstoke: Macmillan.

Järnefelt, E., Zhu, L., Canfield, C. F., Chen, M., and Kelemen, D. (2018), 'Reasoning about Nature's Agency and Design in the Cultural Context of China',*Religion, Brain and Behavior*, 9: 150–78

Johnson, D. (2016). *God Is Watching You*, Oxford: Oxford University Press

Kelemen, D. (1999). 'Function, Goals and Intention', *Trends in Cognitive Sciences*, 3(12): 461–8

Kirk, G. S., Raven, J. E., and Schofield, M. (1983). *The Presocratic Philosophers* (2nd ed.), Cambridge: Cambridge University Press

Kuhn, T. S. (1962). *The Structure of Scientific Revolutions*, Chicago: Chicago University Press

Locke J. (1975). *Enquiries Concerning Human Understanding and the Principles* of *Morals*, L. A. Selby-Bigge (ed.), Oxford: Oxford University Press.

Locke J., (1997, reprinted from 1794 ed., originally published in 1695). *The Reasonableness of Christianity*, Bristol: Thoemmes Press

Locke J. (1997). *Political Essays*, M. Goldie (ed.), Cambridge: Cambridge University Press

Mawson, T.J. (2018). *The Divine Attributes*, Cambridge: Cambridge University Press Elements

McGrath, A. (2019). *The Territories of Human Reason*, Oxford: Oxford University Press

McKim, R. (2019). *Religious Diversity and Religious Progress*, Cambridge: Cambridge University Press Elements

Mill J. S. (1962). 'On Liberty', in *Utilitarianism*, M. Warnock (ed.), London: Fontana

Mulgan, T. (2015). *Purpose in the Universe*, Oxford: Oxford University Press

Nietzsche, F, (1961). *Thus Spake Zarathustra*, Harmondsworth: Penguin

Plantinga, A. (2015). *Knowledge and Christian Belief*, Grand Rapids, Grand Rapids, MI: Eerdmans

Rea, M.C. (2018). *The Hiddenness of God*, Oxford: Oxford University Press

Romero, M. (2018). *Introducing Intersectionality*, Cambridge: Polity Press

Taliaferro, C., and Teply, A. (2004). *Cambridge Platonist Spirituality*, New York: Paulist Press

Trigg R. (1973). *Reason and Commitment*, Cambridge: Cambridge University Press

Trigg, R. (1989). *Reality at Risk: A Defence of Realism in Philosophy and the Sciences* (2nd ed.), Hemel Hempstead: Harvester Wheatsheaf

Trigg, R. (2000). *Understanding Social Science* (2nd ed.), Oxford: Blackwell

Trigg, R. (2014). *Religious Diversity: Philosophicaland Political Dimensions*, Cambridge: Cambridge University Press

Trigg, R. (2015). *Beyond Matter: Why Science Needs Metaphysics*, West Conshocken, PA: Templeton Press

Trigg R. (2017). Does Science Undermine Faith? London: SPCK

Trigg, R., and Barrett, J., eds. (2014). *The Roots of Religion: Exploring the Cognitive Science of Religion*, London: Routledge

Vattimo, G. (2016). *Of Reality*, New York: Columbia University Press

Cambridge Elements ☰

Religion and Monotheism

Paul K. Moser

Loyola University Chicago

Paul K. Moser is Professor of Philosophy at Loyola University Chicago. He is the author of *The God Relationship; The Elusive God* (winner of national book award from the Jesuit Honor Society); *The Evidence for God; The Severity of God; Knowledge and Evidence* (all Cambridge University Press); and *Philosophy after Objectivity* (Oxford University Press); co-author of *Theory of Knowledge* (Oxford University Press); editor of *Jesus and Philosophy* (Cambridge University Press) and *The Oxford Handbook of Epistemology* (Oxford University Press); co-editor of *The Wisdom of the Christian Faith (*Cambridge University Press). He is the co-editor with Chad Meister of the book series *Cambridge Studies in Religion, Philosophy, and Society.*

Chad Meister

Bethel University

Chad Meister is Professor of Philosophy and Theology and Department Chair at Bethel College. He is the author of *Introducing Philosophy of Religion* (Routledge, 2009), *Christian Thought: A Historical Introduction*, 2nd edition (Routledge, 2017), and *Evil: A Guide for the Perplexed*, 2nd edition (Bloomsbury, 2018). He has edited or co-edited the following: *The Oxford Handbook of Religious Diversity* (Oxford University Press, 2010), *Debating Christian Theism* (Oxford University Press, 2011), with Paul Moser, *The Cambridge Companion to the Problem of Evil* (Cambridge University Press, 2017), and with Charles Taliaferro, *The History of Evil* (Routledge 2018, in six volumes).

About the Series

This Cambridge Element series publishes original concise volumes on monotheism and its significance. Monotheism as occupied inquirers since the time of the Biblical patriarch, and it continues to attract interdisciplinary academic work today. Engaging, current, and concise, the Elements benefit teachers, researched, and advanced students in religious studies, Biblical studies, theology, philosophy of religion, and related fields.

Cambridge Elements $\equiv$

Religion and Monotheism